Miracles

Miracles:
A 21st Century Interpretation

Josef Imbach

Templegate Publishers
Springfield, Illinois

Originally published in German as
Wunder: Eine existenzielle Auslegung
by Echter Verlag Würzburg in 1995
English translation by Jane Wilde © 1999 Templegate Publishers
First published in the United States of America by:

Templegate Publishers
302 East Adams Street
Post Office Box 5152
Springfield, Illinois 62705
217-522-3353
www.templegate.com

ISBN 0-87243-239-4
Library of Congress Catalog Card Number: 98-60894

Cover: Detail of Poussin's *Christ Healing the Blind,* the Louvre, Paris

Manufactured in the United States of America

CONTENTS

PART TWO
MIRACLES FROM THE NEW TESTAMENT

Chapter 1
SINKING INTO THE VOID

Chapter 2
LAW OR JUSTICE?

Chapter 3
"YOU GIVE THEM SOMETHING TO EAT"

Chapter 4
OF DEVILS, DEMONS AND EVIL SPIRITS

Introduction

Healing miracles or manifestations, like poems, stories and plays, must be interpreted before they can be understood correctly. The more we concentrate on power, proofs, manipulation and magic, on medical and scientific data, the less we are able to grasp the miracle's spiritual content. If we can just accept that there is such a thing as miraculous healing - in the sense that we discover faith and trust in a power that transcends our own understanding - is it then so difficult to accept a sea change that culminates in psychological or even physical gifts?
J. Cornwell, Mächte des Lichts und der Finsternis. Christliche Wunder - Wahrheit oder Einbildung? Vienna, 1991, 228.

The miracle, faith's dearest child.
J.W. von Goethe, Faust I, verse 766.

"The marriage of Cana - I cannot believe it!" said someone to the great Jerome, "what an immense amount of wine!" The bible scholar replied thoughtfully: "Yes, and we are still drinking from it".
L.Zenetti, Die wunderbare Zeitvermehrung, Munich 1983, 12.

Today miracles are not often discussed. People point out that what seemed miraculous yesterday is now explicable. They see the world as a closed whole, understood by laws of causality. When the inexplicable - therefore "the miraculous" - occurs, they *still* have to search for unknown causes.

This means that even the majority of Christians can no longer see any "proofs" of the truth of Christian faith in miracles, especially as we are now aware that the phenomena generally described as "miracles" are also common to other religions.

My book takes these difficulties into account. The first part deals with the various genres of miracles, with examples from non-Christian and Jewish stories from antiquity and the great world religions, where miracles hold a firm place in man's religious traditions. Part I also has a short digression on a few necessary dogmatic considerations. Part II examines the understanding of miracles in the Bible, with emphasis laid on the New Testament. This procedure makes it possible to demonstrate the religious and historical links that are needed if biblical accounts of miracles are to be understood.

To a certain extent Part II examines examples; I try to bring out the unusual quality of a number of these miracles passed down to us by the evangelists. It becomes clear that in the end all Jesus's works and signs aim at *liberating* us - a liberation *from* guilt, *from* evil, and *from* sin, but also a liberation *towards* self-acceptance, *towards* freedom, *towards* faith, *towards* following him, *towards* joy and life. In other words, Jesus is never concerned simply to heal a person's bodily sufferings, he also tries to bring his whole life back onto the rails again, so that he can find his way to God and to himself.

This means that the reader is not only confronted with the religious message of the New Testament miracles, but simultaneously gains insight into the arduous and yet exciting work done by exegetes and researchers.

In spite of all my efforts to use a language that everyone can understand, it was not possible to avoid some theological terms. There is a list of these at the end of the book. A few years ago I analyzed three of the miracle stories dealt with here in my book "Jesus Begegnen. Biblische Erfahrungen Heute" (Zürich, 1992) But there I was dealing with them in a different context, so there need be no fear of repetition.

Most of the theories propagated here were tried out in two seminars, organized by the Catholic Academy in Augsburg. I was invited to give these by the Director of the Academy, Dr. Franz-Xaver Spengler, and without his initiative this book would never have been written. I owe him a thousand thanks, and also have not forgotten the warm welcome he gave me, nor the friendship he has shown me over the years. I would also like to thank Imelda Casutt for her hard work correcting the galley proofs, and Dr. Michael Lauble for his careful editing.

Rome, January 1995.   Josef Imbach

Part One
Records of Miracles in Religions

1

The Blind see, the Lame walk and the Dead rise

The Typology of Miracles

In Bruce Marshall's delightful novel "Father Malachy's Miracle" a chaplain says "Miracles are quite out of fashion today. If one were to happen in my Lord Bishop's bedroom, his Lordship would do everything to hush up the impertinent event."[1] In quoting this, I have no intention of giving the chaplain a bad name nor of treading on the Bishop's toes. But I think there is something to be said for the author's point of view. Anyone today who seriously believes in miraculous wonders is usually considered "wondrous strange" himself.

Bruce Marshall's illustration of modern man's refusal to acknowledge miracles is both witty and ingenious. The main character in the story is the pious Father Malachy, who has actually performed a miracle himself. During a foggy night the town's notorious dance hall, considered by many a breeding ground for vice, is crushed by a single rock. But the population has no real desire to reform, and does not want to believe in the miracle. Instead people talk about tricks and deception, superstition, psychoses and mass hallucination. The media gets involved, and the dance hall is turned into a nationwide attraction. A wily entrepreneur wants to know about the hall's owners and their contracts; he hopes to get literary and film rights to this so-called miracle. Instead of bringing the people to their senses, this intervention triggers even greater disbelief. A depressed

Father Malachy turns to God for the second time, and begs him to reverse the miracle. One morning, when the dance hall is found to have been suddenly restored to its former place, all the people agree that they have been the victims of collective self-deception.

The events in Bruce Marshall's novel are indeed rather exaggerated. But this applies to any satire. Nowadays people everywhere have become so skeptical about miracles that many refuse even to discuss them.

At best we still use the term "miracle" in its other sense - as Sarah Leander does in the famous old film "Great Love". Some of us still remember her hit song "I know that one day a miracle will happen". We dream of winning the lottery, or large sums of money, or great happiness. It's not difficult to believe in such miracles, because secretly each one of us hopes for them.

Healing Miracles

In a narrower sense, miracles are mostly found within a religious context. There are numerous accounts of supernatural events, for example, proof of divine grace granted to people in a hopeless situation. Many of us spontaneously think first of the *healing miracles* in the gospels.

But those of us with some knowledge of ancient cultures are aware that belief in miracles was also widespread among the pagans in antiquity - and that pilgrimages are not a Christian invention. Votive tablets expressed gratitude to the gods when prayers were answered. Most of our information comes from the archeological findings near Epidaurus in the north east of the Peloponnesus. Today bus-loads of tourists visit this site to see the most perfectly preserved Greek theater of the ancient world. Even more popular is the shrine dedicated to Asclepius, the God of healing, which lies ten kilometers further inland and dates from the fourth century BC. During the 2nd and 3rd centuries AD this god was revered throughout the Roman Empire under the name of Aesculapius. The votive tablets excavated in Epidaurus confirm that people made similar requests to Asclepius as the faithful do today to the Mother of God in Bavarian Altötting or in Maria Einsiedeln in Switzerland. They asked for healing from all suffering, comfort in hopeless situations, and hope in extreme misery. Others came with the same kind of requests to the god as centuries later, Catholics came to Anthony of Padua. Now and again we find rather unusual petitions; Asclepius was asked to promote hair growth, get rid of vermin, or help people to find treasure.

In the nature of things, most of the prayers offered up to Asclepius were requests for *healing miracles*. The following votive tablet gives us a good impression of these.

"Pandarus of Thessaly (came into the shrine) with a mole (birthmark?) on his forehead. In healing sleep he saw a vision; he dreamt that the god bound up his forehead with a cloth and ordered him to take off the cloth when he came out of the shrine, and to bring it to the temple as an offering. When day dawned he stood up and took off the cloth and found that his face was free of the mole. He made an offering of the cloth in the temple. It carried the mark of the mole that had formerly been on his forehead.'[2]

According to this, the cure occurred through divine intervention during a visionary dream, whilst the supplicant Pandarus was sleeping in the healing chamber.
Gerd Theißen has done extensive research into healing miracles, and demonstrates that *the raising of the dead* should be included among them: "At one time almost all raisings of the dead by miracle workers in the ancient world

could be understood as the re-awakening of the apparently dead, and further, the typical motifs are the same: as a rule the procedure then (as now) is the transmission of power through touch".[3]

The Hebrew Bible tells us that the prophet Elijah raised up a widow's dead son, and his successor Elisha brought a child back to life (1 Kings, 17,17-24; 2 Kings, 4,18-37). The latter was granted such miraculous power that even a dead man who was thrown into Elisha's grave came to life again.

So Elisha died, and they buried him. Now bands of Moabites used to invade the land in the spring of the year. And as a man was being buried, lo, a marauding band was seen and the man was cast into the grave of Elisha; and as soon as the man touched the bones of Elisha, he revived, and stood on his feet (2 Kings, 13,20f).

It was said of Jesus that he also brought the dead back to life: the daughter of Jairus (Mk. 5,22-24.35-43), the youth of Nain (Lk. 7,11-17) and Lazarus of Bethany (Jn. 11,1-44). According to the Acts of the Apostles, Peter restored a young girl called Tabitha to life in Joppe (Acts. 9,36-43). Paul raised a certain Eutychus from the dead (Acts 20,7-12). (During his sermon this young man went to sleep by the open window and fell from the third floor.)

After reading these examples we should no longer be surprised that similar events have been handed down to us from the pagan religions of the ancient world. It was said of Appollonius, a contemporary of the apostle Paul, that he brought a dead girl back to life.[4] Similar traditions were widespread in Jewish circles.

The Banishing of Demons

The banishing of demons was also closely related to miracles of healing in antiquity. In the latter the healing power of the miracle worker was foremost, whilst the former was concerned with the open struggle against forces hostile towards humankind.

One of the most famous examples of this is in the Book of Tobit[5] when Tobit is advised by the Archangel Raphael to banish a demon before he spends the night with Sarah, whom he is entitled to wed. Sarah was previously promised to seven men who died one after another in the bridal chamber. The narrator puts this tragedy down to the workings of an evil spirit. When Tobit, the eighth bridegroom, enters her chamber, he obeys Raphael's instructions:

"As for the heart and liver (of the fish), if a demon or evil spirit gives trouble to anyone, you make a smoke of these before the man or woman, and that person will never be troubled again (Tob. 6,7.).
As he went he remembered the words of Raphael, and he took the live ashes of incense and put the heart and liver of the fish upon them and made a smoke. And when the demon smelled the odor he fled to the remotest parts of Egypt, and the angel bound him (Tob.8, 2f).

Numerous witnesses tell us that belief in demons was widespread in cultures of antiquity. In ancient Egypt the power to banish evil spirits was attributed to some divinities and even to their statues. We know from an inscription on the Bentresh stele, which can be seen today in the Bibliothèque Nationale in Paris, that this applied to the statue of the god Khons. The monument is from 4-6 centuries B.C. But the event was reported (in writing) at the time of the

Pharoah Rameses II (1290-1224 B.C.) His wife came from
Bechten, which lay on the northern boundary of the empire.
When her sister Bentresh showed signs of madness, Ramses
arranged for the image of Khons, the god of exorcism, to be
sent to his sister-in-law in Bechten:

*"Then the god went to the place where Bentresh was. And
he helped the daughter of the ruler of Bechten. She was
immediately healed. Then the spirit that was with her said to
Khons: You come in peace, you are the great god who drives
out demons......I am your servant. I will go to the place from
whence I came to fulfill your wish..... then the spirit departed
in peace to the place he chose, at the order of Khons, and
the ruler of Bechten rejoiced greatly, and so did all the people
of Bechten."* [6]

We have a vivid description of exorcism as it would have
been practiced at the time of Jesus from the Jewish historian
Josephus Flavius (37/38 -100 A.D.)

*I saw how one of us (a Jew) called Eleazar freed a man
possessed by evil spirits in the presence of the Emperor
Vespasian, his sons, and high ranking and ordinary warri-
ors. This is how the healing took place: Eleazar held a ring
which contained one of the roots given by Solomon under the
possessed man's nose, let him smell it, and so drew the evil
spirit out of him. The man collapsed immediately, and
Eleazar made the spirit swear never to enter men again by
speaking the name of Solomon and the proverbs written by
him. In order to convince those present that he possessed
such power, Eleazar placed a cup or a basin filled with water
near them, and commanded the evil spirit to knock it over
when he left the man, and so convince the onlookers that he
had really gone. This indeed happened, and thus Solomon's*

wisdom and insight were spread abroad. I believe I have to speak about this so that it may generally be known how powerful the spirit of Solomon is, and how pleasing he was to God.[7]

The impression of magic evoked by such descriptions is avoided in the New Testament. It seems that the New Testament authors occasionally interpreted the phenomenon of possession as a symptom of illness. Luke understands Jesus's exorcisms as healing: a great multitude "came to hear him and to be cured of their diseases; and *those who were troubled with unclean spirits* were cured" (Lk. 6,17-18).

It should not surprise us that there are no accounts of the banishing of demons found in the ruins of Epidaurus, or in the remains of other shrines to Asclepius, because the possessed were denied entrance to the temple area.

Instructional Miracles

Some miracles in the Bible lay stress on specific divine demands. We call these instructional miracles. These are often punitive miracles that serve to bring people to their senses. Yahweh permits the death of the child born of the adulterous relationship between David and Bathsheba (2 Sam 11,1-12.26; 2 Sam 12,14). On another occasion he strikes down the people of Israel with pestilence, because David has ordered a census, thus claiming God's ancient right for himself (2 Sam 24,1-18). There is a well-known punitive miracle in the Acts of the Apostles. The narrator's introduction (end of Acts 4) is important. According to it, many members of the early Christian community in Jerusalem pooled their possessions and shared its administration.

But a man named Ananias with his wife Sapphira sold a piece

20

of property, and with his wife's knowledge he kept back some of the proceeds, and brought only a part and laid it at the apostles' feet. But Peter said "Ananias, why has Satan filled your heart to lie to the Holy Spirit and to keep back part of the proceeds of the land? While it remained unsold, did it not remain your own? And after it was sold was it not at your disposal? How is it that you have contrived this deed in your heart? You have not lied to men but to God." When Ananias heard these words, he fell down and died. And great fear came upon all who heard of it. The young men rose and wrapped him up and carried him out and buried him.

After an interval of about three hours his wife came in, not knowing what had happened. And Peter said to her, " Tell me whether you sold the land for so much." And she said, "Yes for so much." But Peter said to her "How is it that you have agreed together to tempt the spirit of the Lord? Hark, the feet of those that have buried your husband are at the door, and they will carry you out." When the young men came in they found her dead, and they carried her out and buried her beside her husband. And great fear came upon the whole church, and upon all those who heard of these things. (Acts, 5,1-11).

Similar stories of punitive miracles are not only confined to the Bible - they were widespread throughout the ancient world. This emerges from the votive tablets unearthed during excavations at Epidaurus. The following text is an example - not only does it have certain parallels with the healing of Pandarus, but also astonishing similarities to the story of Ananias and Saphira.

A certain Echedorus travels to Epidaurus to be cured of a mole. His friend Pandarus, suffering from the same blemish, gives him some money for the temple, hoping in this way to be freed from his own flaw.

Echedorus now had Pandarus's mole as well as his own.
He had received money from his friend Pandarus to make a
donation to the god in Epidaurus. But he did not want to
hand it over but to keep it for himself.
In healing sleep he saw a vision. He dreamt that the god
came to him and asked him whether he had some money from
Pandarus for an Athena statue as a votive offering for the
shrine. But he said he had not received anything like that
from Pandarus; but if the god would heal him he would have
a picture painted as an offering. So the god bound him with
the cloth of Pandarus in sleep, and commanded him to take
the cloth off when he left the room of healing, and to wash
his face at the fountain and see his reflection in the water.
When day dawned Echedorus left the chamber and took off
the cloth that no longer had the sign of the mole on it. But
when he looked into the water he saw that his face had both
his own mole and Pandarus's.[8]

We know from other accounts that a cure sometimes happened through the intervention of the god Asclepius himself during sleep in the healing chamber. Usually however, the suppliant received detailed instructions in a dream, and following these brought about a cure, often in the most natural way. The instructions given to Echedorus, however, do not lead to the healing of his affliction but punish him with a further blemish for his dishonesty.

In all probability this story is a fabrication. Obviously it is based on the account of Pandarus's healing. This is then re-worked as a frightening example for those who are exposed to temptations like those of the unhappy Echedorus. The moral cannot be misunderstood: it warns pilgrims not to keep gifts dedicated to the gods for themselves, at the same time encouraging them to make a material contribution to the temple thus giving the god due thanks for his healing.

Punitive miracles have a firm place in the religious traditions of the ancient world.[9] Astonishingly enough, no miracle of this kind has come down to us from Jesus - unless we count the rather puzzling episode of cursing the fig tree that bore no fruit among this category (Mk. 11,12-14). Seen from the perspective of historical tradition, however, we are here perhaps dealing with a distortion of the parable of the unfruitful fig tree (Lk. 13,6-9).

On the other hand, Jesus performed several instructional miracles. An example is the story of the healing of the man with a withered hand. Jesus first asks about the prevailing law. "Is it lawful on the sabbath to do good or to do harm, to save life or to kill?" (Mk. 3,4).

Instructional miracles are not exclusive to the New Testament. We only have to remind ourselves of Pythagoras's miracle of the fishes (c.570-c.497 B.C.) He predicts the exact number of fish in a catch to prevent them from being killed.

"And something astonishing happened: no fish that stayed out of the water died while he was counting them. He reminded the people present about their former life, that their souls had already lived once before they became imprisoned in their bodies.[10]

This miracle obviously served to emphasize Pythagoras's theory of the transmigration of souls, on which he based his counsels for a vegetarian way of life.

In Judaism instructional miracles (at least after the destruction of the Temple in 70 A.D.) were not significant. The standard of ethical behavior alone conditions the interpretation of laws handed down, rather than a new revelation, even one followed by a miracle. When the famous Rabbi Eliezer called for a voice from heaven to explain the current practice, he was confronted by another instruction from the Talmud "We are not interested in some sort of a voice because we have already had our directions from Mount Sinai".[11]

Affirmative Miracles

Some instructional miracles are characterized by the fact that they do not emphasize the divine origin of a specific standard of behavior, but try to make us believe in a person's divine mission. This is why we speak of *affirmative miracles*.
So Yahweh commanded Moses and Aaron to reveal themselves to the Pharaoh by working a miracle.
And the Lord said to Moses and Aaron "When Pharaoh says to you, 'Prove yourselves by working a miracle', then you shall say to Aaron, 'Take your rod and cast it down before Pharaoh, that it may become a serpent'". So Moses and Aaron went to Pharaoh, and did as the Lord commanded; Aaron cast down his rod before Pharaoh and his servants, and it became a serpent. Then Pharaoh summoned the wise men and the sorcerers; and they also, the magicians of Egypt, did the same by their secret arts. For every man cast down his rod, and they became serpents. But Aaron's rod swallowed up their rods (Ex 7,8-12).

It is worth noting that Israel's adversaries and enemies also perform miracles, but they are exposed as deceptions. Miracles that only "show off" are no affirmation of divine mission. If there is any doubt about their validity, they have to supply further proof; after all they could have been done with the help of some demonic force or other! In the account above, Aaron provides further evidence by winning the competition between the miracle workers.

Affirmative miracles of this nature have been passed down by many outstanding religious personalities, especially founders of religions. Astonishingly enough, this phenomenon is also widespread in Islam, although the Koran attaches no worth to the evidence of miracles. (Surah 6,111; see also 17,97; 10, 96-97; 6,25). This stems from the Islamic understanding of God's workings. In contrast to our western conception of the natural laws (*behind* or *in* which the faithful perceive the workings of God), classical Islamic theology traces every event *directly* back to God. What man experiences as the law of nature is in reality nothing other than a disposition of God. Although interrupting this disposition *seems* to constitute a "miracle" to the observer, it is just as normal as every other event in the way of the world *according to God's nature*, and is totally directed by him.

However, it does happen that God sometimes acts slightly against his dispositions in order to give us a nudge, especially when he wishes to affirm the authority of individual prophets. With regard to Jesus, the Koran mentions a whole number of such signs: he is born of a virgin, is able to talk in his cradle, makes full-fledged birds out of clay; he heals lepers and the blind and brings the dead back to life. But all these things are worth nothing - even the concept "miracle" - according to the subtle speculations of Islamic theologians. However, the Koran does refer to the fact that these events happen expressly by God's will, so that Allah alone is the originator of such wondrous doings (Surah 5,110).[12] In fact the prophets can only work "miracles" with God's permission. (Surah 40,78; Surah 13,38).

On the other hand, many parts of the Koran stress that God expressly refused to confirm the mission of the last and greatest prophet, Muhammad, through affirmative miracles (Surah 6,9; Surah 17,90-93). But paradoxically Muhammad's first biographer, Ibn Ishaq, tells us of his wondrous signs. Pious Muslims took up the theme; over the course of time Muhammad was credited with many new miracles. They mostly deal with healing or the punishment of opponents - their horses stumble when they pursue him, their hands wither when they try to stone him, they die after he has prophesied their deaths. A purely formal observation of these unusual signs puts them into the categories of healing and punitive miracles. But contrary to all the Koran's reservations mentioned above, they actually function as affirmative miracles.

The same is true of other significant religious personalities like Buddha (6th or 5th century B.C.), or Zarathustra (6th century B.C.) who reformed the ancient Persian religion. Obviously every religion has a tendency to strengthen the authority of its founders or reformers through miracles of proof. It is therefore not surprising that Jesus's numerous symbolic actions become affirmative miracles in the evangelists' way of presenting them.

Epiphany Miracles

In some respects every miracle represents an appearance of the divine. But we actually refer to miracles of *appearance* or *epiphany* when the divine *personally* manifests itself to man. The description of God appearing on Mount Sinai is one of the best examples of this:

On the morning of the third day there were thunders and lightnings, and a thick cloud upon the mountain, and a very loud trumpet blast, so that all the people who were in the camp trembled. Then Moses brought the people out of the camp to meet God; and they took their stand at the foot of the mountain. And Mount Sinai was wrapped in smoke, because the Lord descended upon it in fire; and the smoke of it went up like the smoke of a kiln, and the whole mountain quaked greatly. And as the sound of the trumpet grew louder and louder, Moses spoke and God answered him in thunder. (Ex 19,16-19; see also Ex 3,1; 1 Kings 19,11-18; Is 6; Ezek 1).

Among the epiphany miracles in the New Testament (Jesus's baptism, Mk 1,10-11; Jn 1,32f; and his transfiguration, Mk 9,2-8) the appearance of the resurrected Jesus has particular significance.

Epiphany miracles are also found in non-christian religions. The ancient Greeks reckoned with divinities (Asclepius, Apollo, Zeus) showing themselves to man. At the time of the Ptolemys in Egypt (323-30 B.C.), where the ruler was considered an incarnation of the godhead, official royal visits to a town were compared to a divine appearance, and the epiphany of the divine was taken for granted. This belief was also widespread in Assyria and Babylon and the rest of the ancient world. It included visions (seeing a divinity) and auditions (hearing a divine voice). The Talmud tells us about the latter in the story of the famous Rabbi Aqiba who suffered martyrdom under the Romans in 135 A.D. The episode bears a slight resemblance to the baptism of Jesus and of his transfiguration.

When they took Rabbi Aqiba out to execute him it was the hour of professing the Schema of Israel ["Hear O Israel", the profession of faith in the daily morning and evening prayer (Dtn 6,4). As they combed his flesh with iron combs he took upon himself the yoke of the ruler of heaven (he who prays the Schema of Israel confesses himself to the one God and thereby takes the "yoke of his ruler" upon himself]... a kind of voice came down and spoke: "All is well for you

Rabbi Aqiba, for you are destined for life in the world to come!"[13]

Rescue Miracles

Numerous *rescue miracles* are found in all religious traditions. They tell us how people in danger, in the face of threatening forces of nature or hostile pursuit, can experience unexpected divine help. In the Talmud there is an account of a miracle at sea which reminds us somewhat of Jesus calming the storm (Mk 4,35-41).

A Jewish child found himself on board a gentile ship that was sailing on the Mediterranean. When a great storm rose everyone stood up and raised their hands high and prayed to their own gods without success. When they realized that they were not being helped they said to the Jewish boy: "Child, get up and call to your god, for we have heard that he answers you when you cry to him, and that he is strong. Then the child got up immediately and gladly, and he prayed. The Holy One - may he be praised - listened to his prayer, and the sea was stilled.[14]

Similar traditions of miraculous rescue from shipwreck are found in ancient Greece, Rome and Egypt. These are normally stories of prayers answered by the gods, whilst the New Testament account of the storm ascribes divine powers to the miracle worker Jesus himself.

Gift Miracles

In contrast to rescue miracles, which are always about averting danger, *gift miracles* tell us how people are unexpectedly showered with material goods. The prophet Elijah provides meal for a widow in Zarephath while the country around is in a state of famine (1 Kings 17,8-16; 2 Kings

4,1-7). Muhammad's disciples credit him with similar abilities. The following example comes from a manuscript written by Qadi Jjad in the 12th century and tells of the prophet's numerous miracles already listed in older sources.

Aiijub prepared dishes for the Prophet and Abu Bekr, enough for both of them. Then the Prophet said to him: "Call thirty distinguished men of the town who are not Muslims to come here!" He did this, and they all ate and some food was left over. Then the Prophet said "Call sixty more to come!" And they ate too, and still some food was left over. None of them departed without embracing Islam and paying homage to the Prophet. Abu Aiijub said "180 men ate of my dishes".[15]

Christian readers will remember that Jesus exhibited similar miraculous powers; we are reminded of the feeding of the five thousand with some bread and a couple of fishes (Mk 6,30-44; also see 8,1-10); the changing of water into wine (Jn 2,1-12) and the rich catch of fish (Lk 5,1-11; Jn 21,1-14). These gift miracles in the gospels are characterized by Jesus acting unobtrusively. His works are not the result of requests, and there is no hint of a magical performance. Admittedly there is an obvious reason - people are hungry, the wine has run out, the fishermen's efforts have been in vain. But the miracle itself is quite unexpected.

Typology as an aid to understanding

Only a religious and historical comparison allows us to weigh up the individual miracle traditions correctly. It also enables us to work out a typology for the miracles, and to classify them into groups. But such classification is not done for its own sake. It should rather aim at smoothing the way to greater understanding. A few short comments on the New

Testament show that this actually works. Jesus walking on the lake is an *epiphany miracle,* the feeding of the five thousand comes under the category of *a gift miracle,* the calming of the storm on the lake is a *rescue miracle.* Previously all these miracles were described as *nature miracles.*[16] Those formerly depicted as *concomitant miracles* (the heavenly voice at Jesus's baptism, his transfiguration, the darkening of the sun, the rending of the temple curtains, earthquakes and graves opening at his death on the cross, and the resurrection as a visible event) are more understandable if we interpret them as *affirmative miracles.* A proper classification of the literary form of a miracle story smoothes the way to a proper interpretation of its contents. Stories of miracles are similar to other literary works. If we confuse a biography based on fact with a novel, or a historical report with a legend, we not only reveal our helplessness in the face of literary genres and forms, but demonstrate our inability to understand the basic message of such texts.

2
Miracles accepted Yesterday

Detours into Dogma

"We cannot use electric light and radios, nor can we take advantage of modern medical and clinical aids, and at the same time believe in the wondrous miracle world of the New Testament". This quotation is from Robert Bultmann's famous essay on the New Testament and Mythology, written in 1933.[1]

Decisions in Teaching

Since the Enlightenment, belief in miracles has dwindled, even among the faithful. There was a huge reaction to this decline in the teaching of the First Vatican Council, a time when there were many rearguard actions among theologians. In the Constitution on Catholic Faith approved on the 24 April 1870 (*Dei Filius*) the council members declared:

Whoever says that miracles cannot happen, and that all accounts of them - even those contained in the Holy Scriptures - should be classified as fables or myths; or that miracles can never be discerned with certainty, and that the divine origin of the Christian religion cannot be correctly proved through them, shall be excommunicated with the anathema.[2]

In this document miracles and the "inner help of the Holy Spirit" are seen as "external proofs" of the truth of divine revelation.[3]

We must take note of some points if we are to understand the text correctly.

It is quite obvious that the Fathers of the Council reckoned with the *possibility* of miracles by stressing:

1) that only some quite specific events qualify as miracles;

2) that these specific events demonstrate valid proof of the divine origin of Christian revelation, and therefore of the Christian teaching on faith;

3) that God worked miracles in fact.

The Fathers of the Council were primarily thinking of accounts in the holy scriptures. But the question of the historicity of the individual traditions is not touched on.

Here we should remind ourselves that statements always rest on specific assumptions which, as a rule, are not analyzed. For example, no one would deny that water reaches freezing point at zero degrees centigrade. But scientific findings only retain their validity under specifically prescribed conditions. For instance, the freezing experiment only succeeds when it is carried out at sea level. If other conditions are in operation—atmospheric pressure can also be changed artificially!—experimental proof no longer confirms the statement. Naturally the same is true of statements on church teaching. These also rest on quite specific, usually tacit, assumptions. Logically they are therefore only conclusive to the extent that these assumptions—as a rule not further reflected on—are correct.

Similar statements from Vatican I also rest on assumptions about the problem of miracles that were not analyzed further by the Fathers of the Council. Unfortunately they were so enraptured by their fervent apologia that they allowed their opponents - who totally rejected the *possibility* of miracles - to chase after them, in the hope of beating them on grounds of natural science. They all rushed into a theological cul-de-sac!

Problems that arose..

(1) The concept of miracles assumed by the Council Fathers is a problem in itself. They understood a miracle as a supernatural occurrence worked by God, that could not be explained by natural laws. This view is widespread even today. A reputed lexicon defines a miracle as "an event which apparently contradicts the usual course of things or the natural laws."[4] N.B. *apparently,* not *ostensibly*! (If you don't know the difference look it up in the dictionary!)

Even medieval theologians (I refer particularly to St Augustine) knew that inexplicable events only counted as miracles if they could be traced back directly to God. This point needed making, for in those days no one questioned the dark power of demons and spirits, believing that they could be held responsible for some mysterious happenings. People thought that they could distinguish between these demonic pseudo-miracles and God's intervention in the course of events primarily because his works furthered faith. The religious purpose—for example the manifestation of God's glory—also played an essential part. It is self-evident that faith allows the *possibility* of God's intervention; "For with God nothing will be impossible" (Lk 1,37; Gen 18,14; Jer 32,27).

(2) But does the mere *possibility* of divine intervention allow us to conclude that God *in fact* influences the course of events by circumventing the natural laws? Until a few decades ago Catholic theologians, almost without exception, believed that miracles could be relatively easily authenticated; furthermore, they could be proved empirically, because even if they took place outside the *laws* of nature, they were still within the *reality* of nature.

But they were overlooking the fact that a concept of

miracles, in the sense of God temporarily lifting or breaking the laws of nature, tacitly assumes that these laws of nature are known to all of us. During the course of the centuries natural scientists have constantly discovered new laws, and consequently they have had to modify and correct earlier research. Even this simple experiential fact shows that there is no reason to consider this whole area of research closed— on the contrary! When a natural scientist is faced with an unusual occurrence that cannot be reconciled with the natural laws already familiar to him, he is not entitled to assume that this is God's intervention. On principle in his area of research there are no miracles, but unexplainable phenomena, and he must try to solve them. His inability to do this implies the death of his science, and no advance in knowledge. If he is unable to find a solution, he has, from his own scientific point of view, to leave the question open. *As the representative of his subject* he may not talk about a miracle, because he would then be moving into the area of philosophy or religion, and turning God into a "God of the Gaps" for a lack of scientific knowledge. If natural scientists were ever to succeed in solving this problem, God would only lose a little more ground - and this has often happened. Berthold Brecht illustrates God's progressive retreat from the world in his play "The Mother":

Insurance helps when prayer has not helped. You then don't need to believe in God anymore if there is thunder about; but you must be insured. It helps you. If God is then so unimportant, it's to his disadvantage. Then there is hope that when he has disappeared from your fields, he will also disappear from your heads. In my youth people believed faithfully that he sat somewhere in the sky and looked like an old man. Then aeroplanes were invented, and the newspapers said that everything could be measured in the sky. No one spoke anymore about a God who sat in the sky. But still,

34

one often heard people say he was like a gas, nowhere and yet everywhere. But when we read what all these gasses consited of, God was not among them, and he couldn't have existed out of air, because we knew about this too. And so he became thinner and thinner, until, so to say, he evaporated. And now from time to time we read that he is actually only a spiritual condition, and really, that is most suspicious.[5]

Many events believed yesterday to be miracles are today explicable through advances made in scientific research. In fact although we have taken the theory of relativity into account, it has not stopped us believing in miracles. Incidents that have puzzled us - for example, astonishing recoveries from incurable diseases - may one day become explicable, but will this necessarily mean that miracles are not possible? We know something about the effect that body and mind have upon each other. Doctors emphasize that some physical sufferings are caused or triggered by spiritual conflict. Should we dismiss psychogenic healing, which activates spiritual powers within the patient? We know so little about these. It is interesting that it has even occurred to theologians that there is a kind of "miracle boundary" in the area of religion. We know of no example of re-creating matter. For example, no reliable account of a miracle has been passed down to us of an amputated leg growing back again.

Today, faced with inexplicable occurrences, most people appeal to parapsychology rather than seek a religious interpretation. Parapsychology examines phenomena that run contrary to our common experiences, and for which we have no adequate explanation. This is true also of *psychokinesis*, which is the direct effect of psychic powers on material without a physical cause. There is also *extra-sensory perception*, which takes several forms: *telepathy* (the transmission of thoughts, moods, feelings); *clairvoyancy* (the perception of an unknown fact or event); and *precognition* (perception of a future event that cannot be explained by normal circumstances). Parapsychology largely assumes the nature of the power used. *Animism* attributes a living soul to inanimate objects and natural phenomena, while *spiritualism* does not rule out communication with spiritual beings (i.e. the souls of the dead). In each case, research into these areas attempts to bring definite order into the extraordinary. According to Bela Weissmahr "these phenomena play a significant part in our understanding of miracles, because they enable us to question the right of many theologians to make a sharp distinction between miracles and natural phenomena. The boundary of 'what is possible in nature' is essentially greater than is usually acknowledged. In its turn, this should bring about a greater openness in theology towards, for example, the miracles reported in the gospels."[6]

Obviously as we learn more about the world, we believe that God pays more attention to his laws of creation than people imagined in former times, for their views were largely shaped by a mythical understanding of the universe.

Confronted by an inexplicable event a believer is not justified in calling it a miracle *if he implies that it is God's direct intervention in the course of nature's laws.* St Augustine (354-430) supported this rather simplistic view. He perceived in the miracle an event that broke through the laws of nature *familiar to us.* Thomas Aquinas expresses a similar view in defining the miracle as "that which proceeds from God in passing over *causes known to us".*[7] According to these Doctors of the Church the miracle does not contradict the laws of nature. If need be, it can stand in opposition to *what we know of these laws.* When we take this into account, we may also say that the natural scientist has no right to maintain that God does not or cannot intervene *directly* in the course of nature.

36

Unfortunately theologians have allowed natural scientists to call the tune, and in doing this, they have contributed to and sanctioned the latters' rational view of the world. So even they have tended to lose their feeling for the *religious* significance of the miracle.

(3) Quite apart from these problems, the first Vatican Council questioned how far miracles could be seen as proofs of the truth of Christian revelation.

As we have already seen, extraordinary events - it is of no significance whether they are within the laws of nature or not - are a permanent part of all ancient religious traditions. The Fathers of the Council were not entirely unaware of this, but their knowledge was sketchy. They assumed that the miracles in the Scriptures always reflected historical facts, whilst those outside them were fables. Referring to the Bible, they disqualified outside historical material as devilish deception. Prejudice hardened their minds into believing that God's miraculous power only manifested itself in Holy Scripture and within the confines of the Church.

Today there is a growing feeling, even among the "simple faithful", that miracles from non-Christian religions cannot be simply dismissed, for many of them show signs of historical reality. It is not important to ask if these extraordinary events can be explained "naturally". In any case, why should God's greatness only manifest itself in a miraculous way within the Christian Church - or implicitly, only within the Roman Catholic church?[8] Have we forgotten that nearly three hundred years ago Church teaching expressly emphasized that God's grace also has effect *outside the Church*, and that *Vatican II* teaches that truth and holiness also shine forth *in other religions*?[9] Finally, there are good reasons for assuming that very few biblical miracles happened in the manner we have described, and that some of them are not based on historical events. Naturally I am not implying that most of the Bible miracles are fables or myths - which seems to have been the fear of the first Vatican Council; I am much more concerned to work out the *statement* that these accounts *intended* to make. This is a task that present day proclamation and catechesis are just beginning to approach.

3
Faith's dearest Child?

Understanding Miracles in the Bible

Naturally the members of the first Vatican Council believed that the scriptures were written with the intention of spreading and proclaiming belief in God and, in the New Testament, belief in Jesus as the Christ. They also assumed that most biblical writings passed down historical facts in the modern linear way. But at the beginning of this century people realized that the biblical accounts, from their origins to their final versions, had not been handed down in this manner.

Not only History!

We know that the greater part of the biblical texts cover a long *history of tradition*. Some of these were first passed down orally as smaller independent units before they were finally written down.

In exegesis we speak of both the history of tradition and of *the history of editing*. This term implies that the textual units in the books of the Bible were first handed down both orally and in writing, and then collected at a later date; finally they were edited into book form. The last editor's only concern would not have been to rescue a few literary documents from the past for the future. During his work he would have had in mind a particular circle of readers and the questions that occupied them. The past would have been updated and handed down with a view to the needs of the present.

Therefore some of the biblical accounts do not tell us a great deal about the event depicted, but give us insight into the lives of the people concerned, and enable us to come to some conclusions about them. The editing of the texts is conditioned by the time and the situation. This also applies to accounts of miracles. We do not need a great deal of literary acumen to assess them. Let us take the story of the "Plagues of Egypt" (Ex 7-11; 12,29-34) as an example. A short analysis of this text also means that we can catch a glimpse of the interpreters' workshop.

Let's remind ourselves of the story: because the Pharaoh refuses to let the people of Israel out of Egypt, God empowers Moses to inflict the land with catastrophes and so bring the presumptuous leaders to their knees. Moses turns the water of the Nile into blood, frogs infest the country until it stinks to heaven, gnats appear from the dust of the earth, swarms of flies invade the very corners of the royal palace, a cattle plague carries off the animals, the people are infected with boils, hail ruins the crops, locusts devour anything left, darkness covers the earth...Finally the Lord slaughters all the first-born in Egypt starting with "the first born of Pharaoh who sat on his throne to the first-born of the captive who was in the dungeon, and all the first-born of the cattle" (12,29).
If we read this text carefully, we notice that God is sometimes called "Lord" and sometimes "Yahweh". We may conclude from this that the editor has woven at least two different texts with different names for God into one story. We can see this in the description of the first plague.*

*tr. note: in the English Common Bible only the title "Lord" is used for God. In the following quotations from Exodus, I have therefore followed the German and used "Yahweh," where applicable, to clarify the author's point.

Ex 7,14 Then the LORD said to Moses, "Pharaoh's heart is hardened, he refuses to let the people go. 15 Go to Pharaoh in the morning, as he is going out to the water; wait for him by the river's brink, and take in your hand the rod which was turned into a serpent. (compare 7,9).

16 And you shall say to him: YAHWEH, the God of the Hebrews, sent me to you saying: Let my people go that they may serve me in the wilderness; and behold, you have not yet obeyed. 17 Thus says YAHWEH: By this you shall know that I am YAHWEH: behold I will strike the water that is in the Nile with the rod that is in my hand, and it shall be turned to blood, 18 and the fish in the Nile shall die, and the Nile shall become foul, and the Egyptians will loathe to drink the water from the Nile."

19 And the LORD said to Moses, "Say to Aaron: Take your rod and stretch out your hand over the waters of Egypt, over their rivers, their canals, and their ponds, and all their pools of water, that they may become blood; and there shall be blood throughout the land of Egypt, both in vessels of wood and in vessels of stone."

20 Moses and Aaron did as the LORD commanded; in the sight of the Pharaoh and in the sight of his officials, he lifted up the rod and struck the water that was in the Nile, and all the water that was in the Nile turned to blood. 21 And the fish in the Nile died; and the Nile became foul, so that the Egyptians could not drink water from the Nile: and there was blood throughout all the land of Egypt.

Obviously something is not quite right about this text. At first (verse 15) God commands Moses to go to the Pharaoh and to take with him the rod that was turned into a serpent in a previous miracle. But in verse 17 Yahweh says that he himself will "strike" the water with his own rod. In all the accounts of the Exodus out of Egypt it is normally Moses who carries the staff. This implies that here we are dealing with a later insertion. Originally it was simply (v.17): Thus says Yahweh: "I will strike the water in the Nile". In other words, Yahweh announces a plague of fishes; the water will become so foul that it cannot be drunk. One of the editors put the staff in Jahweh's hand - and in the end it is this staff that gives the whole story a bloody turn of events. On the occasion of God appearing on Horeb, Yahweh says to Moses: "So I will stretch out *my hand* and smite Egypt with all the wonders which I shall do in it; after that he will let you go" (3,20). To confirm his promise, Yahweh temporarily turns Moses's staff into a serpent, and commands him to repeat these miracles before Pharaoh (4,2-4). But what will happen if Pharaoh still does not believe that Moses is sent from Yahweh so that he can lead his people to freedom? "...you shall take some water from the Nile and pour it upon dry ground; and the water which you shall take from the Nile will become blood upon the dry ground" (4,9).

Staff, water and blood - these three requisites were taken over and re-arranged in this order by an editor. Moses's miraculous staff becomes Yahweh's staff. There is no more talk of a couple of drops of Nile water, but of *all* the rivers, all the canals and ponds - everything,including the water used daily in wooden or stone bowls in homes. While in an earlier version of the story it was said that the Nile water was undrinkable as a result of the fish dying (v.18), in the later version (which links the final editor with the earlier one) every drop of water in the whole of Egypt is turned into blood (see v.19). According to the final version, this is what causes the plague of fishes (v.20,f).

Every one of the ten plagues could be considered in this

way, and the result would be similar. Depending on when the individual text units were woven together and handed on, 300 to 800 years lie between the oral description of the events and their transcription. When a story is handed down over a long period of time, frequent embellishments complicate the traditional and editorial history until the account finally becomes improbable. To a lesser degree the New Testament has been embellished in the same way.

The Plagues of Egypt are not an historical account; they are a popular story. The number ten, expressing totality in Hebrew thought, is an indication of this. We are reminded of the ten instructions or commandments that Yahweh entrusted to his people! The last editor slotted different traditions into each other, so that he was able to reach the number ten. The narrator (or last editor?) anticipated the complaint that God was not in a hurry to free his people, and put the answer in God's mouth just prior to the seventh plague:

"For this time I will send all my plagues upon your heart (Pharaoh's), and upon your servants and upon your people, that you may know that there is none like me in all the earth. For by now I could have put forth my hand and struck you and your people with pestilence, and you would have been cut off from the earth; but for this purpose have I let you live, to show you my power, so that my name may be declared throughout all the earth. (Ex 9,14-16).

This also tells us what this miraculous story is about: the narrators wanted to extol God's greatness, to praise his glory and call others to believe in his power (compare 7,5). In other words, all these stories of miracles are heavily stamped with the *character of proclamation.*

From the History of Jesus to History with Jesus

This title is relevant to the gospels and to the miracles handed down in them. We should note five points:

(1) the historical origin of these writings;

(2) the fact that some of Jesus's words and deeds are often reported in a totally different context from the original;

(3) the nature of proclamation in the gospels;

(4) the intensity the miracles acquire during the course of time;

(5) the difference between miraculous *events* and miraculous *stories*.

(1) We reach a deeper understanding of Jesus's miracles if we have previously reflected on the individual characteristics of the gospels; the evangelists could draw upon a history of tradition and editing that extended over many centuries. This meant that they were able to work oral and written sources at their disposal into a whole. They showed that they were not only interested in the *history of Jesus* but above all in *history with Jesus;* in the experiences they shared with him and passed on to the new Church because they believed in him.

If we can visualize this traditional and editorial process, we realize that many of Jesus's words and actions in the gospels are no longer narrated in their original context. This fact alone changes them. An example? Both Mark and Matthew tell us of an *unknown woman* anointing Jesus's *head* in the house of Simon the Leper in Bethany. *Some* of those present (according to Mt 26,8: the *disciples*) were indignant because they thought it would have been better to sell the precious ointment and give the proceeds to the poor (Mk 14,3-5; Mt 26,6-9). However, according to John, Jesus stayed in *Lazarus's house* in Bethany. *Mary* anointed Jesus's *feet,* and

Judas objected that the oil should have been sold for the poor (Jn 12,1-5). Certainly all these versions are based on the same episode, but they have been shaped differently, and in the end we have two different accounts.

(2) As the individual evangelists wove various traditions into their manuscripts, it is highly likely that the miracles they recorded did not always appear in the historical context in which they were originally told. According to Mark, the healing of Peter's mother-in-law follows after Jesus has preached in the synagogue in Capernaum (Mk 1,29-31). According to Matthew, Jesus goes to Peter's house after he has healed the centurion's servant. But even when the three synoptics agree with each other, we cannot be absolutely certain that Jesus really worked a specific miracle *within the context passed down by them.* We know that Matthew and Luke used Mark's gospel as a model, and therefore there is a great measure of agreement between the three. But this does not necessarily mean that the tradition Mark followed was a reliable source for repeating events in historical order.

(3) Here we are confronted with the *historicity of Jesus's miracles.* We not only enquire into the *original context* of Jesus's symbolic actions, but also have to ask the basic question, *did Jesus work miracles at all?* And this is not a rhetorical question. As we have already mentioned, the evangelists were interested in the *history of Jesus,* and also in *history with him,* in what they and the new Church experienced through their belief in Jesus Christ. Naturally these experiences of faith also found expression in the gospels.

In practice this means that the gospels are not factual historical representations of specific incidents from Jesus's life, but a reflection of the author's personal faith in Jesus.

In other words, they do not simply *give a report* about specific incidents, but *interpret* the figure of Jesus, and *propagate* belief in him as the Messiah and Son of God. A comparison serves to show what effect these facts had on their descriptions.

A natural catastrophe occurs somewhere in the world. A serious newspaper gives a factual report. It mentions the place where the accident happened, the number of dead and wounded, and the extent of the damage. An eye-witness's description is quite different. It expresses the fear of someone who has survived. And a priest bases his Sunday sermon on yet another aspect. The place where the catastrophe happened is of no importance. Neither is the exact number of the dead and wounded, and if the priest makes a mistake about the extent of damage done, it is of little consequence. His main concern is to say something about the uncertainty of life, and that death comes when least expected.

The evangelists take on the roles of both the priest and the eye-witness, although they do refer to facts. But their main concern is not just giving us historical data. They express their personal consternation, aroused by the person of Jesus. But they also want to encourage their readers to open themselves to similar experiences and follow Jesus. In short, the gospels are not sober records but *witnesses to faith*, written down *in order to lead people to belief in Jesus Christ, or to strengthen them in this belief.*

This means that fact and commentary, that is, Jesus's life and its significance, are closely blended together. The gospels do not only contain *historical truths,* but also *theological statements*, the latter usually presented in the form of stories. Similar to the way Jesus himself told stories to convey a theological truth, (we think of the parable of the Pharisee and the Publican, Lk 18,9-14) the evangelists or other members of the early Church tell stories about Jesus that describe his mission and his significance in the divine plan of salvation. Some of these stories are about the miracles attributed to Jesus. The following comparison shows us that now and again an evangelist embellishes the miracle story he is describing.

Mk 10,46-52	Mt 20,29-34
..and as he (Jesus) was leaving Jericho with his disciples and a great multitude, Bartimaeus, a blind beggar, the son of Timaeus, was sitting by the roadside. And when he heard that it was Jesus of Nazareth, he began to cry out and say "Jesus, Son of David, have mercy on me!" And many rebuked him telling him to be silent; but he cried out all the more, "Son of David, have mercy on me!" And Jesus stopped and said "Call him." And they called the blind man, saying to him Take heart; rise, he is calling you." And throwing off his mantle he sprang up and came to Jesus. And Jesus said to him, "What do you want me to do for you?" And the blind man said to him, "Master, let me receive my sight." And Jesus said to him "Go your way; your faith has made you well." And immediately he received his sight and followed him on the way.	And as they (Jesus and the disciples) went out of Jericho a great crowd followed him. And behold, two blind men sitting by the roadside, when they heard that Jesus was passing by, cried out "Have mercy on us, Son of David!" The crowd rebuked them, telling them to be silent, but they cried out the more, "Lord, have mercy on us, Son of David!" And Jesus stopped and called them, saying,"What do you want me to do for you?" They said to him "Lord, let our eyes be opened." And Jesus in pity touched their eyes,and immediately they received their sight and followed him.

The scene and structure of both accounts are identical, and so is the course of action. We notice that Matthew no longer writes of *one* named blind man, but of two *unnamed* men. Obviously he has extended his model (Mark's gospel). We come to the same conclusion if we compare the two versions of the healing of the man in Gerasa with an unclean spirit. Matthew has two men possessed by demons, while Mark only mentions one (Mk 5,1-20; Mt 8,28-34). If the word falsification comes to mind here, we might as well blame the Etruscans for not having motorways. We may not judge the historiography of the ancient world by modern standards. There are many examples of Matthew's way of working within the context of his times. This does not mean that writers dealt thoughtlessly with their material. They were primarily concerned to produce a *literary* work. We are reminded of Thucydides (c. 460- 400 B.C.) who put such elegant Greek into the mouths of his military commanders in "The History of the Peloponnesian Wars" that if their speeches had actually been delivered, no soldier would have understood them. The writers of the ancient world were happy to exaggerate when they wanted to praise or even idolize a person. Knowing something of ancient literature, we should not be surprised that the authors of the gospels were subject to these exaggerations, but to a far lesser degree. If Matthew doubles the number of those healed in the passages we have mentioned, he only wants to add weight to the *theological statement* that Jesus, per se, is the bringer of salvation.

(4) We must also remember that in recording a miracle for posterity, the author would certainly paint the miracle worker's power in vibrant colors. We saw this earlier in the history of the Ten Plagues of Egypt. Another example is the description of the sun miracle in the Book of Joshua. The people of Israel have conquered five Amorite kings near the town of Gibeon. The narrator lays emphasis on the fact that the sun stayed in the sky until the Israelites had revenged themselves on their enemies.

Then spoke Joshua to the Lord in the day when the Lord gave
the Amorites over to the men of Israel,
"Sun, stand thou still at Gibeon,
and thou Moon in the valley of
Ajalon."
And the sun stood still and the moon stayed,
until the nation took vengeance on
their enemies.
Is this not written in the Book of Jashar? [the Book of the
Just] (Josh 10, 12f).*

*tr. note: In the German translation and in the New Jerusalem Bible it is called "The Book
of the Just." In the Common Bible it is called the "Book of Jashar."

Today we know that "The Book of the Just" was a collection
of songs that has been lost. They are also referred to in
Samuel II (1,18) as the Book of Jashar. But the sun miracle
in the "Book of the Just" never took place. The verses quoted
in the Book of Joshua are from a hymn which praises God's
power and greatness in poetic language. Obviously the
author of the Book of Joshua was taking the skepticism of
his people into account, and saw himself forced to embellish
his description.

The sun stayed in the midst of heaven, and did not hasten to
go down for about a whole day. There has been no day like
it before or since, when the Lord hearkened to the voice of
man; for the Lord fought for Israel. (Josh 10,13f).

It is likely that the author confused a *hymn* on the conquest
of Jericho that was popular at the time with a *factual report*.
This misunderstanding, later to have fatal and long-lasting
consequences in Galileo's trial, is based on the fact that
miracles always appear more wondrous from a historical
distance, and are correspondingly embellished.

49

We also find something of such elaboration in the New Testament. Here are some examples: According to Mark, Simon's mother-in-law who was healed by Jesus "lay sick with a fever" (Mk 1,30). According to Luke, who referred to Mark's source, this becomes a "high fever" (Lk 4,38). In Matthew (8,5-13) and Luke (7,1-10) Jesus heals the *centurion's slave* without entering the former's house. In Luke (7,6) Jesus is "not far from the house". In both descriptions the centurion is sure that Jesus *can heal his slave without having to go into his house.* In John, (4,46-53) who is in the same tradition but wrote his account a few decades later, the subject is *an official whose son is at the point of death* (4,47). Jesus is staying in Cana, where the official from Capernaum looks for him and expressly asks him *to come to him.* Jesus heals the sick boy immediately, this time from a distance of *almost thirty kilometers.*

While the accounts of the synoptic gospels are simply of healing the blind, in John's gospel Jesus gives sight back to a *man born blind* (Jn 9,1-34). In the synoptics Jesus raises the dead daughter of a ruler of the synagogue to life (Mk 5,22-24. 35-43). Luke tells us that Jesus brings back a youth from the dead *when he is being carried out on his bier* (7,11-17). In John on the other hand, Jesus calls Lazarus back to life when he has *already been in the tomb four days,* and his body has started to decay (11,39).

(5) Finally, we must point out here that some New Testament miracle stories are narrated in a well-defined pattern that was widely used in the ancient world. Normally this had three parts:

(a) an *introduction* describing the form of suffering;
(b) the *course* that healing took;

(c) *confirmation* that healing had actually taken place.

The following comparison between a New Testament miracle and a miracle in Epidaurus shows that in many cases, the *structure* of non-Christian and New Testament accounts has many similarities.

Structure	Epidaurus	Mk 1,29-30
The kind of suffering	Alcetas of Halieis was blind.	Simon's mother-in-law lay sick with a fever.
Healing Action	He had a dream. He dreamt that the God came to him and opened his eyes with his fingers. For the first time he saw the trees in the holy place.	They told him (Jesus) of her, and he came to her. And he came and took her by the hand and lifted her up.
Confirmation	When it was daylight he came out healed.	The fever left her; and she served them.

But we should not conclude from these structural similarities[1] that the gospel miracles were simply *adapted* from reports of miracles in circulation at the time and that all of them were just *fabricated*. It is more likely that this "classical" tripartite pattern was imposed on the theme - and that is why it is found on the votive plaques in many places of pilgrimage today.

And in spite of some superficial parallels, the New Testament accounts of miracles differ from similar accounts in pagan antiquity. The latter usually emphasize the pragmatic aspect, the furthering of trust in the godhead, thus contributing to the prosperity of a specific place of pilgrimage. However, the New Testament accounts of miracles are closely linked to *Jesus's proclamation*, and so cannot be understood simply as demonstrations of his divine power.

But as some of the miracle stories in the gospels follow a previous literary pattern, from the historical point of view we have to ask ourselves whether the authors wanted to describe a factual event, or whether they simply used the current form of narrating miracles to emphasize specific characteristic traits in Jesus - perhaps that he was the Lord of creation. Even when we can establish a historical core, we still have to distinguish between the miraculous *event* and the *narration* of a miracle. From here, the question whether Jesus really worked miracles in point of historical fact arises of itself.

Jesus as a Miracle Worker?

During the last fifty years scripture scholars have developed methods that enable us to check theological statements based on historical facts. So in some cases, we can establish whether there is a historical foundation for a specific saying or action of Jesus, or whether we are dealing with an early Christian or evangelistic invention. Unfortunately there is not space enough to go into this in great detail in this book.[2] But most biblical scholars agree that Jesus did in fact heal the sick and cast out demons. Jesus himself substantiates this when he defends himself against his adversaries' reproach that he cast out demons with the help of Beelzebul, the Prince of demons. He exposes the senselessness of this accusation by pointing out that Satan would then be working against himself (see Mt 12,24-28). He continues:

And if I cast out demons by Beelzebul, by whom do your sons cast them out? Therefore they shall be your judges. [They refute your absurd accusation alone by the fact that they too cast out demons without being accused by you of having a pact with Beelzebul]. But if it is by the spirit (Lk: finger) of God that I cast out demons, then the kingdom of God has come upon you (Mt 12,27-8; Lk 11-19f; Mk 3,22).

This saying can be traced back to Jesus - it was not, like many other statements, put into his mouth by the evangelists. Another fact that is often overlooked, even by Christians who know the bible well, is significant here; Jesus openly admits that the sons of his adversaries have healing powers. He is not by any means the only miracle worker in Galilee at the time. For their part, Jesus's adversaries do not doubt that he has cured the possessed. They merely accuse him of having a pact with Satan, and performing his miracles with the latter's help. Jesus, on the other hand, defends himself against this reproach by maintaining that God's spirit works within him.

This whole debate demonstrates at least three things: that at the time everybody was convinced that people could fall into the power of demons; that there were charismatics who were able to free the sick and the possessed from their sufferings; and that belief in healing miracles was widespread in the ancient world. This means that we cannot simply dismiss non-Christian miracles as figments of the imagination, and that historical questions about them are appropriate. Lastly, our text also proves that miraculous healings performed by Jesus have been variously interpreted - his adversaries condemned them as devilish illusion whilst his disciples saw in them a proof of divine power. This does *not* mean that *all* healing of the sick and *all* casting out of devils depicted in the gospels happened in the way we have described. Moreover, we cannot rule out the fact that some of the accounts of miracles have no historical basis, but represent a story-like form of Jesus's message. According to many scholars, this is more than likely. In other words, the historicity of individual healings of the sick and those possessed by demons has to be tested in each case.

As far as the other miracles recorded by the evangelists are concerned (miracles of rescue, instruction, gifts, epiphany or waking from the dead), most scripture scholars hold that these are stories that aim at stressing Jesus's message and his supreme significance for mankind. We most likely do them more justice by reading them as *narrative catechesis*, based on the experience that Jesus is life indeed - and that he gives life to all who follow him.

But we have not yet penetrated to the core of Jesus's statement, which is his own understanding of miracles: *"But if it is by the spirit of God that I cast out demons, then the kingdom of God has come upon you"* (Mt 12,28). In his miracles, Jesus sees a sign and a confirmation that the kingdom of God proclaimed by him has already dawned with his own appearance - and that this kingdom of God is not only of a spiritual or sacred nature, but also affects mans's earthly existence. Besides, he also wants to re-form people through his miracles. This emerges from a passage that is authentically in his own words: "....for if the mighty works done in you [Chorazin and Bethsaida, towns in Galilee] had been done in Tyre and Sidon, [towns that counted as strongholds of godlessness in the threatening words of the prophets; see Amos, 1,9-10; Is 23; Ezek 26-28; Zech 9,2-4] they would have repented long ago in sackcloth and ashes" (Mt 11,21).

The faith that the evangelists proclaim in their writings is the essential faith and has nothing to do with whether individual miracles actually happened as they are described or not. This opinion sometimes exceeds the boundaries of a theologian's understanding, as we can well see from the following statement: "It always seems to me that a pericope like the raising of Jairus's daughter would be uninteresting if it were simply a symbolic story".[3] This pre-empts any historical critique. It should be mentioned here that proof of the truth and the strength of faith are not derived from the miraculous event, but ultimately from the proclaimed message alone. This is only revealed to those who actively imitate Christ. If we think that there is good reason to test the historicity of individual miracles, it does not mean that we do not believe in the gospels. When we approach the texts with watchful eyes and open hearts we shall soon understand that it does not depend upon their being historical or not historical but upon their message. In the following chapters I shall concentrate on this aspect and not on the historical question.

A quarter of a century ago Rudolph Pesch wrote about the historicity of the miracles, and his theses are just as valid now as then:

1) The historicity of the New Testament narration should be proved, not simply assumed.
2) As the techniques of research are so advanced today, the burden of proof falls on those who claim accounts of miracles are sources for the historical Jesus.
3) Without exception, these accounts do not describe the historical course of events. It only makes sense to analyse them for their historical foundations (Jesus's actions, the Christology of the early Church, missionary proclamation).
4) The historical foundations of accounts of miracles can be events from the life of Jesus, but in most cases they are factors of the early Church, although in varying degrees connected to Jesus's life.
The plain distinction of historical or non-historical yields nothing as far as miracles are concerned. Historical reality is reflected in all literature, because this is itself a piece of the same thing.[4]

The behavior of his opponents shows that Jesus's miracles do not represent any "neutral" proofs of the truth of his message. They do not deny his unusual actions; they just interpret them differently - and persist in their unbelief.

Jesus's fellow countrymen in Nazareth also react incredulously to the amazing things that are said of him:

"Where did this man get all this? What is the wisdom given to him? What mighty works are wrought by his hands! Is not this the carpenter, the son of Mary and brother of James and Joses and Judas and Simon, and are not his sisters here with us?" And they took offence at him. And Jesus said to them, "A prophet is not without honor, except in his own country, and among his own kin, and in his own house." And he could do no mighty works there, except that he laid his hands upon a few sick people and healed them. And he marvelled because of their unbelief (Mk 6,2-6).

According to this passage, Jesus refuses to legitimize his mission by miraculous signs. It is possible that the remark about his healing a few sick people can be traced back to the evangelist who wanted to tone down Jesus's lack of success among his fellow countrymen. Matthew 13,58 is similar, although he neutralizes Mark somewhat: "And he did not do many mighty works there, because of their unbelief". Also according to Luke Jesus refuses to perform any miracles to move people to believe in him. When he leaves Pilate and is taken before Herod, the latter hopes to see a miracle because he has heard people talking about them. But Jesus does not even acknowledge him with a word (Lk 23,8-11).

Through his behavior Jesus gives us to understand that his miracles are signs only. They are not meant for admiration, but seek to make us aware of his message and follow him. According to his understanding (and that of the apostles) there is a close link between miracles and faith. But this does not mean that his miraculous actions should lead those present to believe in him. The opposite is true. It is exactly the other way round.

Belief or at least the readiness to believe is the *prerequisite for the miracle*. Jesus did not feel able to work miracles in Nazareth and before Herod because he was up against unbelievers. On the other hand, the evangelists repeatedly emphasize that Jesus talks about the power of faith "participating" when a miracle happens. He often says to those he has healed "your faith has made you well" (Mk 5,34; 10,52; Lk 17,19). This is not to insinuate that faith works miracles, but rather that there are limits set for divine action if the readiness to believe is lacking. Let me put this into everyday language; certainly God *gives* his gifts of faith; but he does not force anyone to *accept* them. So Jesus's miracles are simply an aid to faith, assuming that the person does not set himself against this faith from the beginning.

Although Jesus himself did not credit his miracles with any kind of value as proofs, some of his works in the gospels function as affirmative miracles. John's gospel says: "Now Jesus did many other signs in the presence of the disciples, which are not written in this book; but these are written *that you may believe that Jesus is the Christ, the Son of God, and that believing you may have life in his name"* (Jn 20,31).

This affirming of Jesus's mission is sometimes referred to by an opponent, for example when the demon that Jesus drives out in Capernaum cries out with a loud voice to all those assembled in the synagogue "I know who you are, the Holy One of God" (Mk 1,24). The unclean spirit that Jesus drives out of the possessed man in Gerasa expresses itself in the same way: "What have you to do with me, Jesus, Son of the most High God?" (Mk 5,7).

Sometimes the evangelists affirm Jesus by allowing a story to fade away in a kind of chorus ending. After he has healed a lame man, those present are quite beside themselves: "We never saw anything like this!'' or: ''And they were astonished beyond measure, saying, 'He has done all things well; he even makes the deaf hear and the dumb speak' '' (Mk 7,37).

Jesus's miraculous works are often presented as affirmative miracles *by the evangelists*, because they did not want to confront their readers with the bare facts. Their main concern was to summon them to belief in Jesus as the Christ, and to spread this faith further. It is then self-evident that Jesus's miracles would be given a theological coloring. To put it more precisely: the evangelists' christological interpretation of his person is reflected in the way his miracles are represented.

"Great are the Works of the Lord"

In healing the sick and the possessed from their sufferings it is not necessarily implied that Jesus temporarily suspended some of the laws of nature. As we discussed in the previous chapter, this question has to remain open for purely natural scientific reasons.

In Jesus's time the problem never arose in this particular form. Of course people had experiences different from the common course of things and termed them "miraculous". But they lived in the consciousness of a world entirely ruled and directed by God. Today believers see God as the primal cause (the creator) who works through the secondary causes, the natural laws, a distinction unknown to contemporaries of Jesus who saw God *everywhere* and *actually* at work, even in the most ordinary events of life.

According to the Bible, a miracle is therefore not perceived when *something extraordinary happens*, but where someone *recognizes God's workings* in normal daily events.

Augustine expresses this in one of his sermons: "The ordering of the whole world is a greater miracle than the feeding of the five thousand with five loaves of bread, and yet it does not astonish us; on the contrary, we are astonished by Jesus's miracle, not because it is greater, but because it is seldom".[5] In the same way Jesus simply wants to remind people by his "extraordinary" signs that they should open their eyes and recognize God's workings *everywhere*, even where their ephemeral desires and yearnings are not fulfilled. The whole of scripture bears witness to the fact that human beings can indeed praise God's greatness and his power in all possible situations because they find *all* his works miraculous. According to the Bible, extraordinary events simply remind us that all God's actions towards us are one single miracle.

This understanding of the miracle is newly affirmed by the Church in Vatican II: "God, who creates everything and maintains it through the Word (Note the present tense! Compare John 1,3) bears witness of himself to mankind in all created things (Romans, 1,19f)".[6] The Council repeats in plain language what the psalmist sings from a heart filled with faith "Great are the works of the Lord" (Ps.111,2).

A simple example can show us that modern man is also capable of such religious poetic feeling.

Two people are in love and blissfully happy. Perhaps they met through pure chance. Let's imagine that the girl had to travel to a certain place on a specific day, but missed her train because she overslept. She takes the next train. She ends up in the same compartment as a young man. He is travelling in the same direction, but due to exceptional circumstances, he has taken the train a day earlier than originally planned. During the journey they get to know each other and now they are extremely happy. Is this pure chance? Not exactly, because every chance has a cause. If someone oversleeps there are reasons; perhaps they are overtired, or for certain reasons they forget to set the alarm. And if someone goes on a journey a day earlier than originally planned there are also precise reasons for this. Two people meeting on a train is the result of a complicated chain of cause and effect. In everyday language we call this chance, or destiny. But whom should the two people thank for their good luck?

G. K. Chesterton once said that he could not imagine a worse moment in the life of an atheist than when he has the feeling he must thank someone - and he does not know whom to thank. But a believer knows. He is convinced that God holds *everything* in his hands and also works even when someone is not concerned with him, and is only aware of natural laws. That is why the two people in our story can say: God, how happy and grateful we are that you ordained things for us in this way!

Does this meeting of two people, with a natural explanation, seem less miraculous than the inexplicable healing of the sick? Faust remarked that the miracle is "faith's *dearest* child."[7] Is this relevant here? It has to remain an open question. But it is certain that the miracle is faith's *child* because it is first and foremost faith that perceives God's works in every event.

Yet this faith is not dependent on spectacular miracles. God's footfall and fingerprints can be recognized in all events and in us all. Of course we need faith's magnifying glass to see this. Often God's handwriting is not easy to read, but in fact it can be deciphered everywhere, even in quite ordinary everyday events. And everywhere and always we find the same words: *God loves us.*

God loves us. In fact, this is the only miracle. Everything that we go through, whether it is explicable or inexplicable, is the *result* of this one miracle of God's love. The rose in the garden, the wine on the table, friendship and the trust placed in us by others, the butterfly and the laughter of children - are they not all *wondrous and miraculous*?

Part Two
Miracles from The New Testament

1
Sinking into the Void

Peter walks on the Sea (Mt 14,22-32)

In 1796 the German writer Jean Paul (whose real name was Johann Paul Friedrich Richter) published "Siebenkäs", his most famous novel. Although he had studied theology, he spent his life teaching and writing, and this book is the story of an almshouse lawyer.

The novel contains the well-known chapter on the dead Christ who speaks from the silence of the cosmos saying that God does not exist. The author describes a dream - he finds himself in a church among the dead.

And then a mighty and noble figure sank down in infinite pain from the heights above the altar and all the dead cried out "Christ! Is there no God?"

He answered: "No, there is no God"...

Then Christ continued: " I went through the worlds, I climbed to the suns, and I flew with the constellations through the deserts of heaven; but there is no God. I flew down, as far as existence threw its shadows, and I looked into the abyss, and I called 'Father, where art Thou?' but I heard only the eternal unconquerable storm; and without the sun that had created it the shimmering rainbow of nature arched down over the abyss. As I looked up into the immeasurable world for the divine eye, it stared out at me from an empty fathomless socket; eternity lay on chaos, and gnawed at it and then regurgitated it. 'Scream out you discords' howled the shadows, 'because He is not!...'

Then, a heart-stopping terror, the dead children came into the temple. They had awakened in God's acre, and they threw themselves in front of the lofty figure at the altar and said: "Jesus! Have we no father?" - and with streaming tears he answered: "We are all orphans, you and I, we are without a father"... And as I fell down and looked into the luminous cosmos, I saw the rings of the giant serpent of eternity rising to encircle the world. And the rings fell down and the serpent coiled itself twice about the universe, then wrapped itself around nature, crushing the worlds together and compressing the everlasting temple into a church of God's acre. Everything became narrow, dark and fearful. And as I awoke, an immeasurably long bell hammer was ready to strike the last hour of time, and shatter the cosmos.[1]

The Night of Nothingness

The thought that there is no God is a nightmare for Jean Paul. It is followed by the relief of awakening.

My soul wept for joy at being able to worship God again - and the joy and the weeping and the belief in Him were the prayer. As I rose, the sun shone brightly behind the full purple ears of corn, and sent the peaceful reflection of his evening splendor to the new moon...[2]

Jean Paul's dream simply reflects a believer's individual doubts, not the latent atheism that was to mark the beginning of a new era. The novelist emphasizes this in a short footnote which precedes his vision:

If my heart had once been so unhappy and so deserted that

all its impulses to acclaim the existence of God would have been destroyed, I would have been shattered by my dream and... then it would have healed me and given my impulses to believe back to me again.

There must be many Christians who wish for the calm, relaxed, almost cheerful certainty of faith that speaks from these lines. It seems that believers today are often less able to protect themselves with experiences similar to Jean Paul's. In fact, it is the other way round after Nietzsche proclaimed the death of God. The tortured doubts that Jean Paul, perhaps the most sensitive prose writer of all German classical writers, felt as a mere nightmare, have been bitter reality to many believers. And in contrast to earlier times, the person affirming God is now forced to justify himself, not the person who denies him. The number of Christians openly confessing their struggle with all kinds of difficulties is increasing. Their faith, in the true sense of the word, seems questionable. This causes inner uncertainty and apprehension, and not infrequently, massive guilt feelings. Their desire for a firm and indisputable faith and their search for suitable models are understandable.

Anyone even slightly familiar with the church's calendar of saints might look for example to Saint Thérèse of the Child Jesus. She is represented by some biographers as the modern example of someone with a courageous and steadfast attitude to faith. Even when she was a child - she was born in 1873 - she was so obedient and pious that only the Mother Superior of the Carmelite Convent in Lisieux was surprised when barely fifteen years old, she asked to be admitted. Two of her elder sisters had already taken this step before her, but they were of a more suitable age.

The little Thérèse, as she was called soon after her death (to avoid confusion with the great mystic St Teresa of Avila), lived in Carmel for nine years. She died of consumption in 1897.

She gives us information about her life before and after entering the convent in notebooks that were edited by her sister Pauline who had preceded Thérèse to Carmel and whose name in religion was Mother Agnes of Jesus. Agnes went to the Mother Superior, a rather daring step to take, and told her of these accounts of Thérèse's religious experiences.

No one could have foreseen what would happen then. The small inconspicuous handwriting struck readers like lightning. Thousands and thousands of copies were printed. The book was translated into more than thirty languages. We read that Thérèse already felt herself drawn to "the bridegroom of virgins" at the tender age of two. She is "the little white flower" that Jesus picked and re-planted in Carmel to protect her from "the poisoned breath of the world".[3] We read how sweet it is to throw oneself into Jesus's arms. She wishes to remain unobserved and inconspicuous. She describes herself as "the very small Sister Thérèse".

I am a very small soul, who can only offer dear God very small things. It frequently happens that I let these small offerings that bring the soul so much peace go by; but this does not discourage me; I can bear to have a little less peace, and endeavor to be more awake next time.

And of the consumption that devoured her—*we must bear the sufferings that Jesus sends! She knows that she must die. And the sooner she dies, the sooner she will be united to the heavenly bridegroom:*

The little child Thérèse *knows only one thing - to love you O Jesus. Great works are denied her, she cannot proclaim the gospel nor shed her blood...But how can she show her love, as love can only be proved by works? Well now, the little child will strew flowers, and their scent will envelop the royal throne, and her clear silvery voice will sing the Song of Songs.*

Doubtless the enormous success of this modest manuscript can be explained by the uncertainty of the faithful at that time. The cloister was a spiritual garden, an anchorage in the storms, a shelter from doubts, a fortress of refuge from the unbelievers whose numbers were increasing. It was paradise anticipated.

Somehow all this is too good to be true; it is too sweet, too flowery, too sentimental. We may have an intimation of darkness, but feel too inhibited to express it clearly: Thérèse's "Story of a Soul" is religious kitsch. But *this* "Story of a Soul" was published by Mother Agnes.

Today we know that the Mother Superior had good reasons for not letting the original manuscript out of her hands. But her death in 1951 enabled the scholarly Carmelite monk Francois de Sainte-Marie to get hold of some other rough notebooks that Thérèse had used to write down her experiences in the convent. This proved that the little Thérèse's spiritual autobiography, which had been quoted so often by hundreds of well meaning preachers and "uplifted" thousands of people had been *edited* by her sister and the Mother Superior according to the rules of edifying literature. In this case it had been touched up, censored, and falsified.

During the course of her few years in the cloister the "little white flower" had actually written down some other experiences. Her sketch books not only deal with piety, but also with frightful loneliness, depression, and a "grim dark tunnel" that Jesus lets her pass through. We hear no more about "clear faith", and "thoughts on heaven" which are her "only happiness". It is a fact that at first she simply could not imagine there were people who were godless, without faith. "I thought they spoke against their better judgement when they denied the existence of heaven". At one fell swoop not only her whole world but heaven itself fell apart, when at the request of her sister and the Mother Superior, she admitted writing the notebooks.

During those joyful days of Easter (in 1896) Jesus let me feel that there are indeed souls who do not have the faith... He allowed the most impenetrable darkness to invade my soul; and the thoughts of heaven, so sweet to me, became only the cause of struggle and torture... This test was not to last for a few days or a few weeks, but would only be extinguished at an hour determined by God... and this hour has not yet come.

If I seek rest for my exhausted heart through all the darkness surrounding it in memories of the radiant land (of heaven) for which I yearn, my torment is doubled; as the voices of sinners grow, the darkness seems to mock me and call to me: "You dream of light, of a homeland pervaded with sweet fragrance, you dream of the everlasting possession of the creator, of all these miraculous works! And one day you falsely imagine that you can escape from the dark clouds that surround you! Go on, go on, rejoice in death that will give you, not what you hope for, but an even darker night, the night of nothingness".[4]

This "Night of Nothingness" has been experienced by many of the great mystics - we only have to remember the great reformer of the Carmelite order, St John of the Cross (1542-1591). But they understood it as a time of inner drought and hopelessness, the experience of the *absence of God*. It is different with Thérèse. During the course of a whole year she was constantly overwhelmed by fearful doubts of the *existence of God*. So she shared the burden of modern man completely. She showed that the Zeitgeist had also penetrated the cracks in the convent walls. She is not the small sweet dreamer of Jesus as we have thought of her for so many decades, but a courageous and tested saint. Modern people can identify themselves with her, in her doubts about faith, her fears and depressions. Hans Urs von Balthasar was right when he wrote that the now *complete* edition of "The Story of a Soul" has lifted Thérèse "out of a cosmetic tomb".[5]

In fact, the uncensored writings of St Thérèse enable us to see all her other notebooks in a new light. They are an impressive document of how threatened faith actually is, and that it has to prove itself anew at every point of time and in every situation. But then, doubt and threat are part of faith's inner nature.

Peter and Endangered Faith

The New Testament gives us a moving and stormy scene on the Sea of Galilee (Mt 14,24).

Then he made the disciples get into the boat and go before him to the other side, while he dismissed the crowds. And after he had dismissed the crowds, he went up on the mountain by himself to pray. When evening came, he was there alone, but the boat by this time was many furlongs distant from the land, beaten by the waves; for the wind was against them. And in the fourth watch of the night he came to them, walking on the sea. But when the disciples saw him walking on the sea, they were terrified, saying "It is a ghost!" And they cried out for fear. But immediately he spoke to them, saying, "Take heart, it is I; have no fear." And

Peter answered him, "Lord, if it is you, bid me come to you on the water." He said "Come." So Peter got out of the boat and walked on the water and came to Jesus, but when he saw the wind, he was afraid, and beginning to sink, he cried out, "Lord, save me." Jesus immediately reached out his hand and caught him, saying to him, "O man of little faith, why did you doubt?" And when they got into the boat, the wind ceased. And those in the boat worshipped him, saying "Truly you are the Son of God" (Mt 14,22-32; compare Mk 6,45-52).

From a literary point of view this is the story of a miracle in which elements of stories of appearance (epiphany) and revelation are melted together. But the actual theme is the nature of faith. Using this example of the apostle Peter, who he believes will play an outstanding role within the church, Matthew explains that no believer can ever exclude the possibility of his faith weakening. It was Peter who proclaimed Jesus Messiah and Son of God in his act of faith in Caesarea Philippi, a town situated about twenty kilometers from the north shore of the Sea of Galilee (Mt 16,13-20), and it was Peter who spoke for the disciples (Mt,17,24-27). Although he was the first among the apostles to reveal his doubts (Mt 14,31), he should not really be held up as an example of this, only in so far as his behavior is exemplary because the evangelist uses his person to illustrate what no believer should forget. At times he will lose his faith, and this also means losing the ground under his feet.

We can no longer be certain whether the episode of Peter walking on the water was invented by Matthew himself and whether he then inserted it into Mark's gospel - which was his model - or whether it can be traced back to an older tradition. But the very fact that Matthew inserted this story, leads us to conclude that he wanted to link it to a quite specific theological message.

We know that people only find each other through trust. And without this trust we can find no support in Jesus. As long as we rely upon ourselves alone we are ground-less in the literal sense of the word, thrown about by the foaming waves of life. At the mercy of every wind, we are in danger of drowning. We distrust everyone. When the disciples see Jesus they are terrified because they think he is a ghost; they cry out in fear. It is only after Jesus invites them to "Take heart" that Peter dares to say a word and finally to take a step - and here Peter does represent the faithful. But as soon as he concentrates on himself and therefore on his weakness and frailty, his trust sinks, and so does he. Again he calls out, still from fear, but this time to *someone*: " Lord, save me!"

This short episode from Matthew's gospel teaches us about faith. By "faith" most people understand a kind of assumption or opinion which rests upon reasons that are not sufficient in themselves to promote a secure (and that means evidential) statement.

Such an understanding of faith is linked to the fact that since the beginning of modern times, religious faith has been defined with an eye to exact, scientific knowledge, whose findings can be proved empirically. Within this framework, religious faith of necessity must appear as a kind of scientific *substitute*. But we must remind ourselves that in practical life, statements that can be proved are not decisive, but rather those truths that we can *merely* attest to, and these are worth living *and* dying for. It is doubtful whether anyone would give his life for the statement, based on scientific fact, that ice begins to melt when the point of zero is reached. On the other hand, many people were prepared to suffer a painful death rather than burn some incense sticks before the statue of a god. They never considered for a moment whether their attitude could be proved scientifically. Such reasoning would be just as impossible as proving that it is better to choose good rather than evil. Aristotle (B.C.384-322) had already pointed out that anyone who believed that he was allowed to murder his mother would not deserve refutation but rebuke.

A simple example illustrates that decisive truths in our lives are not based on scientific knowledge, but on experience. When a person says to another, "I like you, I'm fond of you, I love you" this statement can change the other's life fundamentally, although there is no - and cannot be - empirical proof for such remarks. Theoretically there is no way of excluding with any mathematical certainty the possibility of being deceived. And yet it can be that we are so sure of the love of another person that we never even entertain thoughts of deception. This is not because love is blind, but because there is a cognition beyond scientific knowledge that grows from trusting contact with others. Insights gained in this way are certainly not *substitutes for knowledge but another kind of knowledge* that develops within us out of an *inner certainty.*

According to the scriptures, this kind of inner certainty also applies to faith. When the subject is faith in the New Testament, this concept is first and foremost unshakable trust in Jesus Christ, through whom God comes closer to humankind. This is all that Matthew illustrates in his story of Jesus and Peter meeting on the Sea of Galilee. At the same time he emphasizes that such trust is not given once and for all and then forgotten, but must be practiced anew and lived anew. This is the reason why no one can ever maintain that he or she finally has faith. It is actually a matter of realizing and deepening this trust each time.

Although faith, like a decision, has to be declared "once and for all", we have to renew it daily. To a certain extent there are no final decisions because we are always living in them - we are constantly faced with new *decisive situations*. A woman celebrating her silver wedding or a monk the golden anniversary of his profession may well ask whether the earlier decisions made once and for all were the right ones. Even if they both come to the conclusion that in spite of all incoherences and all failures they still stand truly by their vows and will continue to profess them, they are not simply repeating an earlier decision but making a new one that is in harmony with it. Our example shows that decisions one makes "once and for all" must be repeated over and over again in concrete circumstances.

This also applies to faith, where relapse is also possible, as the - by no means exemplary - example of Peter shows. He had hardly taken the force of the wind into account when his trust was overwhelmed by fear, and he began to go under. If we want to understand the text, we must not confuse cause and effect. Peter is not afraid because he goes under, but because and to the extent that he fears, he begins to sink into the waves. And this is most certainly not the last time that the apostle goes under. During the last supper he actually swears to Jesus "Even if I must die with you I will not deny you" (Mt 26,35). Only a few hours later, overcome by fear, he curses and swears to a pair of curious idlers that he does not know Jesus (Mt 26,69-75). The believer should not undervalue the dangers to faith. Like human trust, trust in God is at the mercy of vacillation, subject to doubts and threatened by crises. All this was in the evangelist's mind when he wrote down the episode of Jesus walking on the water and Peter's sinking into the waves. He wanted to strengthen and encourage believers, aware of their ambiva-lent situation and possibly suffering from it.

Unfortunately I cannot avoid a few illustrations from biblical interpretation to support this. Scripture scholars draw our attention to models for Jesus walking on the water from the Hebrew Bible, where on several occasions the subject is passing *through* water: the Israelites crossing the Red Sea (Ex 14,21-31); the chosen people crossing the Jordan (Josh 3-4); Elijah crossing the Jordan (2 Kings 2,7f.14). But none of these examples is about walking *on* the water, an image that first appears in the Book of Job: "who (God) alone stretched out the heavens and trampled the waves of the sea" (9,8).

In the ancient world (especially the world outside the Bible) walking on the water was considered a divine gift, and there are many examples in literature of this, apart from the passage in Job mentioned above. In the pagan world this ability was mostly attributed to sons of the gods (heroes) or to men who had a special relationship to the divinity.[6] There are also parallels to the story of Peter walking on the water in Buddhist traditions, more precisely in a jataka.[7] This one is about a lay brother who is on the way to his Master on the banks of a river. The ferryman has just gone, and so the brother "moved by joyful thoughts of the Buddha" puts his foot on the water and begins to walk over the river. "But as he reaches the middle, he sees the waves. His joyful thoughts on the Buddha weaken, and his feet begin to sink into the river. But then he awakens even stronger thoughts about the Buddha and goes on, over the surface of the water".

Of course the striking similarity between this episode and the story of Peter does not prove that there is a direct link between both stories, but it illustrates that the theme of walking through and on the water (and of flying, by the way!) was certainly not only confined to the Bible, but was something which fascinated the whole of the ancient world. This is not without significance for Matthew's description of Jesus on the water. In fact, it seems that the evangelist is not trying to depict *a factual event*, but using a *concept widespread at the time,* in order to make a *theological*

75

statement.

The disciples' boat is far from land, more than several hundred meters. (We know that a football stadium, depending on the size of the sports center, is between 185 and 193 meters long.) Besides, there is a strong headwind. Jesus is not there; he has gone up into the hills to pray in the loneliness of the night. The disciples have been left alone because Jesus himself has sent them off. He only approaches them again during the fourth night watch, that is, between three and six in the morning. They have been fighting the waves almost all night. But they do not see *him*; they think he is a ghost. What they do not yet know is that *he sees them.*

In all probability, the evangelist is drawing upon the experiences of his contemporaries, who believed in Christ but were haunted by dark doubts. He would have used the motif of walking on the water, well known at the time in the Jewish and Gentile worlds. This assumption becomes more probable if we compare the Matthew pericope with Mark's text which was its model (Mk 6,45-52). Mark has simply handed down an account of a miracle. He wants to show that Jesus is also Lord of natural forces, or as we would say today, cosmic laws. According to his version, Jesus intends to pass by the disciples but because they are beside themselves with fear he gets into the boat with them (Mk 6,48-51).

Matthew adds the story of Peter walking on the water to the text that he has taken over from Mark. He shows that Jesus is near his followers even when they no longer think he is there. Actually, it implies even more - it means that against all appearances they can always rely on his beneficial presence. At the same time Matthew emphasizes that we overlook Jesus being with us the moment we fix our minds solely upon ourselves. This remains a problem for us even today.

We often hear people complaining loudly that they cannot

experience God, that he does not reveal himself but seems absent. In the person of Peter, the first among the apostles, Matthew shows that this impression has nothing to do with the present-day lack of belief. It seems that this experience is part of the very nature of faith.

For this reason the Mother Superior of the Carmelite convent in Lisieux showed how utterly blind she was; otherwise it is difficult to explain why she censored precisely those passages in Thérèse's autobiography with which so many of the faithful can identify today.

The character of Pastor Helander in Alfred Andersch's novel "Zanzibar or the Last Reason" represents this absence of faith. He is in charge of a small parish in Rerik, a dreary little town on the Baltic. As the thugs of the Third Reich become more audacious, Helander decides to arrange for the statue of a monastic student reading a book to be sent abroad, to save it from the National Socialists. In their eyes it is degenerate art (the author had a sculpture by Ernst Barlach in mind). The Pastor is entirely alone. His parishioners have either come to some arrangement with the new rulers, or they have gone over to join them. Ever since they did so, the church has been dead. It even seems as if God himself is withdrawing from the scene. Helander only experiences him as "the absent one", as *Deus absconditus*.

Somewhere he had read that engineers could now build "soundproof rooms". That was the right description. The town, the church, the parsonage, they had all become soundproof, rooms without echo, since the others had conquered. No, it wasn't since the others had come, it was since God had distanced himself.[8]

The Church in Crisis

Matthew faces a similar situation. He has noticed that many of his companions are uncertain about their faith. Christ seems to have distanced himself from them, and the faithful are thrown in upon themselves. In contrast to this painful experience, the evangelist emphasizes that Jesus is also present even if he seems to be absent. And this situation is a challenge for the faithful. It is not by accident that Matthew gives Peter the entire stage - we have already established that the latter has a position of prime importance in his gospel.

In this sense, the meeting of Jesus and Peter on the Sea of Galilee is not only of prime importance for the faith of the individual, but also for the faith of the whole church. Peter does not only appear as an individual in this episode; he is also the exponent and representative of the whole church. We notice this in Matthew's gospel because whenever he mentions Peter, he does not only focus on him alone, but on the whole Christian community (Mt 16,16-20; 17,24-27; 18,21-23). In the figure of Peter walking on the water Matthew emphasizes that the church will always feel abandoned when she forgets that Jesus is permanently with her on her journey.

This is first mentioned when Jesus tells his followers to get into the boat while he ascends the mountain to pray. He has distanced himself from them. In a sense, they are embarking on a kind of independent venture of their own. This can be seen as anticipating the disciples' situation after his death and resurrection. The Master has absented himself from his community; he has become *invisible*. His followers forget all too easily that he who has risen is still among them. This leads us to the story of the calming of the storm (Mt 8,23-27), which reminds us that Jesus is stronger than any threat from within or without. We can assume that the episode of his walking on the water is an adaptation or a continuation of the story of calming the sea. Both stories are about fierce winds and waves. This imagery represents the young Church, confronted by hostilities from without and threats from within. On her passage through time the ship of the church is tossed about by headwinds and waves. All effort and all commitment can so easily seem in vain, the forces of chaos appear stronger, and the crew - the community of faith - starts to panic.

The chosen people have a similar experience when they leave Egypt. At first everything seems to go well. Yahweh, the savior, the God of liberation, does not abandon his people. He breaks the Pharaoh's will, he leads his people on showing them the way in a pillar of cloud by day, by night in a pillar of fire (Ex 13,21). But as soon as the first difficulties appear—bitter undrinkable water (Ex 15,23), shortage of food (Ex 16,3), shortage of water (Ex 17,1f)—the people falsely imagine that they have been abandoned by God. Hope of a bright future vanishes, as does their faith in Yahweh, the liberating God. The people yearn for conditions they found intolerable only a short time ago. "Would that we had died by the hand of the Lord in the land of Egypt, where we sat by the fleshpots and ate bread to the full" (Ex 16,3).

Both the Hebrew Bible and the New Testament show that the community of the faithful have to reckon with difficulties, and because things go wrong or fall by the wayside, their faith in the Lord weakens or disappears.

The history of the Church is a history of one crisis after another, always followed by fresh attempts at overcoming them in a constructive way. One of the first crises within the early Christian church is mentioned in the Acts of the Apostles. The argument was about the Jewish law of circumcision - should it also be applied to Gentiles who had converted to Christianity? The report of the Apostles' Council reveals the extent to which this confrontation threatened their very existence; they were only able to agree after "...Paul and Barnabas were drawn into a great controversy with them." (Acts 15,2)

Shortly afterwards the faithful became increasingly anxious because the Second Coming which they had at first thought of as imminent (Mt 16,28) was continuously delayed. The delay of the Parousia was the source of ridicule and derision, even among the earliest Christians, as we can read in Peter's second letter (3,3-10) which was actually written by an anonymous author in the middle of the second century.

A further crisis in the church loomed in the year 313, when the Emperor Constantine's "Edict of Milan" came into force. Although this gave religious freedom to Christians previously persecuted in the Empire, it also bestowed a variety of privileges on them, so that some people were converted for selfish reasons rather than religious convictions. The questionable alliance between the throne and the church has its roots here. In the future, the church was to attach great worth to this alliance, thus undermining the credibility of its proclamation.

Only a short time later the struggle to pass along orthodox teaching - especially in the area of Christology - threatened to tear the Church apart. The burning question was how much freedom of conscience and action the Church authorities could allow the faithful, without threatening the unity of faith. In fact the Church had to face severe tests of tradition and doctrine, for example at the beginning of the 13th century when the growing schism between the Eastern and Western churches became final; when the churches in the Reformation allied themselves against Rome; and when the opponents of the dogma of infallibility left the Roman fold and formed their own churches.

Perhaps one of the most dangerous crises during the whole of church history until the present day was provoked by the Enlightenment in the 17th and 18th centuries, when the broadly held view was that man only had to answer for his thought and action before the Altar of Reason. Totally unprepared for this challenge and incapable of dealing with its complexities, the Church began to condemn all enlightened thought. As a result, she provoked the serious Modernist struggle at the turn of the 19th and the beginning of the 20th centuries. All the theologians who strove for reconciliation between Catholic belief and modern thought - most of them involved in philosophy, historical research and biblical interpretation - were branded as *Modernists*, accused of heresy and condemned by the Roman authorities. A good many of their questions were justified. They were not answered, simply repressed. We should not be surprised therefore that they surfaced again during the 1950's. Church authorities spoke contemptuously of a *nouvelle théologie*, whose representatives - Henri de Lubac, Yves Congar, Marie-Dominique Chenu - were silenced by the old and well-tried measures of disciplinary action. From the Church's point of view, no crisis was *permitted*. Instead of mature considerations there were immature reactions. It becomes clearer every day that Vatican 11 was the first Council to bring about immediate changes, which questioned the reasons for the previous crises honestly, and looked for solutions to them.

Our cursory overview shows that to a certain extent the story of Peter's walking on the water anticipates the whole future history of the Church. This pericope has not lost one jot of its immediacy as long as the Church seems to prefer burying her head in the sand when faced with difficulties to fixing her gaze faithfully upon Christ, who alone protects his people from downfall. Peter's story expressly reminds us that the actual danger to the faithful lies in the fact that they forget that they *are on the way*, and that Jesus accompanies them upon this way.

This is the aspect that Vatican II repeatedly emphasizes about the Church. Referring to the chosen people of Israel crossing the desert, in words full of imagery the Council describes the search for "the coming and eternal city" (Heb 13,14).[9]

According to the hopeful words of the Council's Decree on Ecumenism, the people of God "although during their earthly pilgrimage at the mercy of sin, grow in Christ, and are gently led by the mysterious will of God, until they come with joy to the fullness of eternal majesty in the heavenly Jerusalem".[10]

Do we have to emphasize further that the Church will always have to struggle with difficulties, whether they come from within the community of the faithful, or whether they come from outside? Like it or not, crises are part of the life of the Church.

Naturally people who only see the negative in every crisis prefer to deny this. But a crisis is simply a challenge that confronts us and has to be coped with. When two people suddenly realize that their marriage is in difficulties, it implies that many things once taken for granted, have now become unbearable. They must be questioned and revised if possible. Perhaps the couple have started to live separate lives almost without realizing it; perhaps they have forgotten that a relationship between two people does not function of its own accord. Old habits and intimacies have to be examined.

There are various ways of reacting to such a situation. Some of us panic. Others think - this can't be true! We refuse to recognize that we have sometimes been wrong. But we can also question the reasons for this crisis, and search for a way to overcome it. A crisis often turns out to be an important moment in the process of maturing.

These points also apply to the crises in the Church. If they can be overcome and not repressed, they can both strengthen and renew the community of the faithful. Whether the Church represents a *community* of the faithful or does not is shown at the moment when members and leaders of the Church can summon up the courage to admit to a crisis, and then confront it. The fifteenth chapter of the Acts of the Apostles serves as a model for this. Whenever there is a lack of courage there is also a lack of faith in Jesus being nearest to his own, precisely when they are faced with difficulties. And these can only be overcome if Jesus's followers do not cast an anxious eye on the "Zeitgeist", but turn their gaze towards him, as he calls to his disciples when he meets them at night on the Sea of Galilee, "Take heart, it is I; have no fear".

The message of the story of Peter's walking on the water has been decoded: if God chooses not to protect his Church *before* a crisis, she may still count on his assistance in *all* the dangers that follow.

2
Law or Justice?

Healing of the Man with theWithered Hand
Mk, 3, 1-6

People are quick to look to the law when they feel threatened by another person's behavior. They pore over clauses, scrutinize paragraphs, look for loopholes. Their rights are lawful, and indeed they refer to lawful rights. If they can get away with it, their *sense* of Justice has been gratified, although *Justice* herself often falls by the wayside.

The difference between law and justice is almost as great as the difference between a comedian and someone who writes comedies. The actor can misrepresent the playwright's ideas in a hundred ways - just as the principle of applying justice can lead to injustice crying to heaven. The ancient Romans formulated this succinctly as *summum ius - summa iniuria*, which means that a pedantic use of the law can sometimes result in great injustice. Friedrich Dürenmatt illustrates this paradox in a story that might appear frivolous at first sight.

The Caliph Harun al Rashid and his Grand Vizier were greatly threatened by the Christians, because the Christians knew that enjoying alcoholic drinks before a battle meant they could work themselves into a fury during the battle, and gain an easy advantage. The Caliph and his Grand Vizier made up their minds to get to the bottom of all this scientifically, and obtained permission from an interpreter of the law

84

to drink some bottles of Chateau-neuf-du-Pape that they had plundered.

After they had drunk three bottles, they were able to dispose of Christian war tactics, and their conversation, without their knowing quite why, turned to women. The Grand Vizier owned a beautiful slave girl, and the Caliph demanded her as a present. The Grand Vizier swore by the Beard of the Prophet that he would not give away the slave. The Caliph offered to buy her. The Grand Vizier, strangely obstinate, which was not usually his way, swore by the Beard of the Prophet not to sell her. After two more bottles of Chateau-neuf-du-Pape, the Caliph also swore by the Beard of the Prophet that he would own the slave that very night.

He had hardly uttered the oath before they stopped and stared at each other, for they had both sworn the opposite of what the other had sworn by the Beard of the Prophet. They asked for the resident scholar to be called, and he came lumbering in, rather sleepily, because he too had been allowed to partake of some bottles of Chateau-neuf-du-Pape for the purpose of study.

The Caliph and the Grand Vizier explained their dilemma to the scholar. He yawned. "Great Caliph" he said, "the problem can be solved easily. The Grand Vizier should sell half of the slave to you, and give you the other half; then he will not have broken his oath, because he swore by the Beard of the Prophet not to sell or give away the whole slave."

The scholar was rewarded with a hundred gold pieces and went off home. The Caliph and the Grand Vizier drank another bottle of Chateau-neuf-du-Pape, and the slave girl was summoned. She was so beautiful that the Caliph swore he would sleep with her this very night - unfortunately once more by the Beard of the Prophet. The Grand Vizier grew pale, took the cork out of another bottle of Chateau-neuf-du-Pape for scientific purposes, and babbled: "Great Caliph, *you have sworn something new and impossible by the Beard of the Prophet, for the slave is still a virgin, and according to the Law, you may only sleep with her after rites have been performed over several days." The Caliph, filled with consternation, asked for the scholar to be called again. The Scholar of the Law, awakened for the second time, listened to this new mishap. " Great Caliph" he said, "Please call for a slave." A slave was called and tremblingly paid obeisance to the Caliph. "Give the girl to this slave as his wife", commanded the scholar. The Caliph obeyed. "Now" continued the scholar, "the slave shall express a wish to divorce himself from her. You must arrange the divorce, and according to the Law, you may sleep with a divorced woman."*

But the slave girl was so beautiful that the slave refused to divorce her. The Caliph offered him pieces of gold, but in vain; the slave remained obdurate. The scholar shook his head. "Great Caliph" - and he yawned sorrowfully - "how scant your knowledge is. Nothing can stand up against our Law. Two ways are open to you. Hang the slave. You may go to bed at any time with a widow. The widow of a hanged man is without honor." "And the second way?" asked the Caliph. "Make a free woman of her" commanded the scholar. "Be a free woman" said the Caliph. "You see," confirmed the scholar, "now you can divorce her from the slave against his will, for she is a free woman and he is a slave, and a marriage between a free person and a slave girl, or a marriage between a slave and a free woman can be dissolved at any time, without even considering how much further we are able to go with our social order. Now I'm finally going off to sleep."

The scholar was rewarded with a thousand gold pieces, paid his respects, and removed himself from the company. The Grand Vizier had already dozed off, and was carried back to his palace. In spite of everything, the slave was hanged, and the Caliph Harun al Rashid was left alone with the beautiful slave girl, now a free woman, and the last bottle of Chateau-neuf-du-Pape.[1]

The Moral of the Story

This is obviously a fictitious story told by a non-Muslim with a faulty knowledge of Islamic teaching but it can serve our purposes here if we remember that a similar distortion of Christian legalism might be as readily invented. Three points are worth noting.

1) It goes without saying that a thorough knowledge of the law can bring about some perfectly legal judgments.

2) But is everything that seems *right* always *just*? Returning to our story, we would have to ask whether a law that makes a distinction between slaves and free men can be consistent with human rights and therefore with justice? Obviously some principles of law rest on cultural, social or religious assumptions. These must be examined too, particularly when they treat people like objects.

3) This story could seem somewhat bawdy; but the point of the story is not that the Caliph wants to sleep with a beautiful slave girl. We are disturbed because the scholar's sharp observations do not rest upon any order of law devised by man, but upon his interpretation of the religious laws. This means that they lead back to Allah himself, partly directly, partly indirectly, depending on whether they are dealing with instructions in the Koran, or with the legal principles derived from them. By calling upon God and his revelation, it seems that one can gain any number of advantages as long as one has the necessary theological knowledge.

Possibly Christians tend to shake their heads when they think about such a murky state of affairs - and that is good.

But if they do this, they should remember that there were always different Muslim schools of law, and that Islamic law has gone on developing over the course of time. And it should not be forgotten that many of the laws in Christianity once in force are not pleasantly remembered today because they represent an obvious violation of human dignity. There are many examples, but perhaps it is enough here to mention the Constitution *Ad exstirpanda* of 1252, where Pope Innocent IV gave the inquisitors power to use torture in extorting confessions.

In contrast to *religiosity*, which can also be lived *individually*, *religion* is a *social phenomenon* that rests upon shared convictions, rites and institutions. These enable its adherents to determine their position in the world, and express their hopes. Besides, every religion gives its members certain norms of behavior and expects them to observe these laws if they are to achieve the goals the religion has set. There really is a law based on religion. It is not our task here to debate the question of why different religions do not agree with each other about specific things - for example, is divorce forbidden or allowed? Our real concern is with the principles of law, sometimes postulated by the religions, that stand in unbearable contradiction to the justice they proclaim.

Does Man live for the Sabbath?

Let us keep this contradiction in mind as we read the following, rather shorter story.

Again he (Jesus) entered the synagogue, and a man was there who had a withered hand. And they watched him, to see whether he would heal him on the sabbath, so that they might accuse him. And he said to the man who had the withered hand "Come here." And he said to them "Is it lawful on the

sabbath to do good or to do harm, to save life or to kill?"
But they were silent. And he looked around at them with
anger, grieved at their hardness of heart, and said to the
man "Stretch out your hand." He stretched it out, and his
hand was restored. The Pharisees went out, and immediately
held counsel with the Herodians against him, how to destroy
him (Mk 3,1-6).

We do not need to be an investigative reporter or a rocket
scientist to understand. Jesus's question "Is it lawful on the
sabbath to do good, to save life or to kill?" We do not have
to be theologians to know it is a rhetorical question.

A story culminating in such a succinct sentence is called an
apothegm. The word is of Greek origin and means a "terse
saying." This definition of the literary form of the word
clarifies the evangelist's intention; he is not concerned with
an historically accurate representation of a specific event,
but with Jesus's succinct words on the meaning of the
sabbath. The rest of the story also draws attention to these
words.

The Pharisees behaved strangely. How did they know that
Jesus was going to heal on the sabbath? According to Mark,
Jesus's public life had only started a short time ago, and in
Capernaum he had once freed a man from an evil spirit on
the sabbath. There were obviously no Pharisees present on
this occasion (Mk 1,21-28). But they could always have
heard about his healing on the sabbath. If so, did it give them
adequate grounds for thinking of Jesus as a persistent of-
fender? Maybe we should assume that Mark later post-dated
the alarming confrontation between Jesus and the Pharisees?
Maybe he could have had good reason; at the very beginning
of his gospel Mark had stressed an important matter that
concerned Jesus - and himself. The miracle was simply the
frame or illustration serving his purposes. Possibly he was

inspired by a punitive and healing miracle from the Book of Kings. There a Man of God is the subject; he threatens King Jeroboam (931-910) with the law because the King has erected an altar to a golden calf in Bethel, 18 kilometers north of Jerusalem.

And he (the Man of God) gave the sign the same day, saying "This is the sign that the Lord has spoken: 'Behold, the altar shall be torn down, and the ashes that are upon it shall be poured out.'" And when the king heard the saying of the Man of God, which he cried against the altar at Bethel, Jeroboam stretched out his hand from the altar, saying "Lay hold of him." And his hand, which he stretched out against him, dried up, so that he could not draw it back to himself. The altar also was torn down, and the ashes poured out from the altar, according to the sign which the Man of God had given by the word of the Lord. And the king said to the Man of God, "Entreat now the favor of the Lord your God, and pray for me, that my hand may be restored to me." And the Man of God entreated the Lord; and the king's hand was restored to him, and became as it was before (I Kings 13,3-6).

The similarity between this and Mark's account of Jesus's miracle - the hand stretched out - makes us wonder if the evangelist's story has a historical basis. Lack of source material prevents us from answering this question, but it is no longer significant, because, as we have already seen, the whole story merely provides the frame for Jesus's words about the meaning of the sabbath. This is the point of the story. And we cannot understand the scope of his remarks if we do not have a certain knowledge of the background to the religious history.

At the time of Jesus most of the Bible scholars were united in the belief that God simply wants the well- being of humankind, and that his will is expressed in the Ten Commandments, which are also the core of the Covenant between him and his people. To be accurate, the Hebrew word for "commandment" which is *debarim* (plural of *dabar*), must be translated as "words". This original meaning has been preserved in English from the Greek as "decalogue": the ten words. The negative overtone that the word "Commandment" has in our ears is not there in the original, and neither are the ten repetitions of "you shall/shall not." The exact translation is "you will/will not." God simply maintains what is actually self-explanatory; his directions are not stumbling blocks along the way towards him, but milestones to becoming a happy and effective human being.

From the introductory: "And God spoke all these words, saying 'I am the Lord (Yahweh) your God who brought you out of the land of Egypt, out of the house of bondage. You shall have no other Gods before me" (Ex 20,1f; compare Deut 5,6). It is quite clear that God trusted man with his *instruction* for his own good - the word is used even today in Judaism. At first God reminds his people that he has stood by them in the past, and indicates that the instruction is only there for their good.

At the time of Jesus the Pharisees, the scripture scholars and other religious groups and communities, hoped to bring about the rule of God through meticulous observation of the law. Judaism has 365 bans and 248 commandments that are still observed by orthodox Jews today. These more or less cover all the important situations in life, and it is easy to understand that there is not a lot of scope left for independent action. Besides, initially it was far too much for these simple people, mostly illiterate, to absorb 613 directions, let alone to cope with interpretations that are often extremely subtle. Those who did not know the instruction and the religious law that stemmed from it were naturally unable to obey them;

such people were considered sinners and impure.

It is only with this background in mind that we can understand unusual questions like "Who is my neighbor?" (Lk 10,29) or "Lord, how often shall my brother sin against me, and I forgive him?" (Mt 18,21). There is little fantasy or spontaneity if love is defined by laws! When we remember this, the very thought of love representing the true criterion for interpretation of the law must simply appear as *the* ultimate heresy.

But this is precisely what Jesus teaches. The evangelists never tire of emphasizing how vehemently he turns against the superficiality of religious regulations. He does not want to abolish them; he wants their real meaning understood (Mt 5,17). This applies as much to directions of the law (Mk 7,10-11) as it does to the strict laws of cleanliness (Mk 7,15) and the casuistic statutes (Mt 23,16-22). Jesus does not dismiss the law; he merely puts it in proper perspective.

His attitude to the sabbath makes this particularly clear. According to the witness of all the evangelists, this attitude is not only there to foster agreement, it soon leads to serious conflicts, particularly with the Pharisees. Jesus does not question the sabbath as such. He wants to liberate this day from all casuistic petty-mindedness and go back to the original definition of the word as "a delight" (Is 58,13), a space where man can praise God without pressure and enjoy his rest without constant fear of breaking regulations.

The Tables of the Covenant (Ex 20,22-23,33), dating from about 900 B.C, state that the sabbath was simply a day of rest for man and beast (Ex 23,12). During the Babylonian exile in 600 B.C., it became Israel's "declaration of faith", in the midst of a Gentile world. Not observing the sabbath was considered a falling off, punishable by death (Ex 31,12-17). This was the start of the rigorous instructions about the sabbath.

Naturally Jesus accepted the sabbath as holy (Ex 20,8). The day may not be profaned by work or business (Ex 20,10; compare Is 58,13). But he did not want to be involved in the laws derived from God's original instruction, and the fear of the sabbath that arose from them. For "the sabbath was made for man and not man for the sabbath" (Mk 2,27). At Jesus's time it seems that this was no longer taken for granted.[2] The rabbis had thirty-nine main activities and a number of lesser ones that were forbidden on the sabbath. Isaiah had warned the people not to leave their houses to *"pursue your own business,"* and from this came the later commandment not to walk more than a thousand ells (some versions say two thousand). The authorized sabbath day's journey (Acts 1,12) was five hundred to a thousand meters. No one was allowed to carry anything or to cook—food had to be prepared the day before—or to pour water into a jug. Some interpreters of the law not only forbade people to help their cattle at a birth, but also to have sexual intercourse and bowel movements. The sabbath - a day of delight?

The Pharisees show how strict the sabbath rules were by reproaching Jesus when his disciples plucked a few heads of grain on this day. This counted as one of the lesser activities linked to the main activity of harvesting (Mk 2,23). If the disciples had known or been warned about this before, they would have been stoned for desecrating the sabbath (according to the contemporary interpretation of Num 15,32-36). At the time of Jesus the rabbis were arguing among themselves about permission to comfort mourners and visit the sick. The school of the famous and compassionate Rabbi Hillel (c. 20 B.C.) allowed this, while the no less famous but merciless Rabbi Schammai (c.30 B.C.) forbade it. The Talmud instructed that no doctor could be called to aid a sick person on the sabbath, unless he were in danger of death.

For some schools within contemporary Judaism these

regulations are not relics of a distant past. In contrast to liberal reformed Judaism, which tries to keep pace with the times, they play quite an important part in both Orthodox Judaism, which simply ignores what is modern, and in conservative Judaism, which tries to coexist with modernity.

However it is not only strict Jews but also fundamentalist Muslims who wonder why some Christians distance themselves from the norms of behavior in the Talmudic instructions. Catholics all too easily and happily forget that they themselves are hardly entitled to mock a rigid interpretation of Jewish and Islamic religious laws. In the Canon law published on January 25 1983 we come up against the most bizarre acrobatics in interpretation, no different from the casuistry of the Talmud. I give just two examples. We know that the priest celebrates the Eucharist standing. But because some priests suffer from old age or illness, the Church is faced with the burning question of how to act correctly in such situations. Her considerations appear in the first paragraph of Canon 930: " a sick or an old priest unable to stand may sit while he celebrates the Eucharist in compliance with the liturgical laws; but he may only celebrate in public if he has his Bishop's permission." Current church law permits exceptions to many regulations if these can be justified by an "appropriate reason" (*iusta causa*). In the case of receiving holy communion however, the law says succinctly: "Those who wish to receive communion must refrain from eating or drinking with the exceptions of water and medicines, for at least an hour before" (Canon 919 par.1). Only these two exceptions are permitted. A singer in the choir who sucks a sweet during the sermon, so that his voice will not let him down in his solo during the preparation for the offering, may not receive communion.

Finally we must remind ourselves that the numerous regulations and rules we find merely curious today were

94

accepted and practiced without question over the centuries. People were threatened with hell fire if they ate a cheap sausage on a Friday, but enjoying an epicurean fish dish did not bar your way to eternal bliss. Are we not reminded of civil law when we think of applying penitential regulations in this way? We all know that civil law also has some "dirty tricks" up its litigious sleeve. In a similar way interpretation of church law sometimes threatens to degenerate into an art form, allowing every pleasure without forfeiting heaven.

Testing by Example

It is natural that followers of every religion ask themselves - or should - how they can apply the enforced norms of behavior to a particular situation. The pharisaic interpretation of Jewish religious laws was *originally* aware of this. In reality the Pharisees were not the somber characters that appear in the gospels. Jesus was actually closer to their way of thinking than to any other religious group within Judaism at that time. In contrast to the Sadducees, who recruited their followers from members of the temple aristocracy, the Pharisees were a lay movement supported by the middle classes. Most of the Bible scholars belonged to this. Both the tradition of the elders and the Mosaic law were binding (Mk 7,3.13). Constant study and considerable scholarship were required. According to the Pharisees, only people scrupulously observant of the law and tradition were pleasing to God. The Pharisees had a very special reason for continually thinking up new and specific provisions and working out ingenious regulations that took every possible situation into account, so ordering all the various parts of life down to the minutest detail (just remember the rules of the sabbath, that seem so grotesque to our eyes). *To start with* these new instructions formed a kind of *protective wall or fence*, erected around the sabbath so that it could not be abused (Ex 20,8: "Remember the sabbath day, to keep it holy."). But this laudable view failed to the extent that numerous protective paragraphs gradually began to take on a life of their own, and were no longer a help but an unbearable burden.

Jesus, who saw through all this, wanted to restore the sabbath's original significance. Of course this day is dedicated to God (Ex 20,10), but the oldest reason for resting on the sabbath was actually social: "Six days you shall do your work, but on the seventh day you shall rest; that your ox and your ass may have rest, and the son of your bondmaid, and the alien, may be refreshed" (Ex 23,12). In short, the sabbath should be blessed so that people can feel well and enjoy themselves in the presence of God.

It was Jesus's attitude towards the sabbath, among other things—and here we are on historical ground—that first led to controversy with the Pharisees, and finally to open confrontation. It is not hard to understand why the evangelists handled them without much goodwill. But we can assume that only a few of the Pharisees co-operated with the supporters of the ruling house of Herod to get Jesus out of the way.

Of course the confrontation between Jesus and the Pharisees was not only about the sabbath. This was simply the material that Jesus used to explain his attitude towards the *whole* of the law. There is a particular reason why this led to such conflict. It was not only the (religious) law but its *interpretation by the rabbis* that were, for the Pharisees, the foundations of every discussion. Here were principles that they could hold onto. Here a path had been prescribed, and they could take it in safety. Here they were not faced with making awkward decisions. Here there was nothing to analyze, and questioning their own responsibility was unnecessary.

But when someone suddenly appears, admittedly not to

question the law, but the whole "tradition of the elders" (Mk 7,3,13) with its "ifs and buts", its "perhaps and in case of doubt", its "however and yet nots", and he simply maintains that it is enough to grasp the original intention of the laws, of course the quibblers and the casuists cannot go along with him. Typically enough, the Pharisees' argument only moves within the casuistic framework. This is the framework that Jesus wants to explode. It is not the law that is the center of his argument, but the well-being of humankind.

"Come here," says Jesus to the man with the withered hand. We can only evaluate the episode if we have understood the symbolic nature of this command. The man represents the *person crippled by the law in his humanity*. Bound by norms that are no longer questioned, his actions and the unfolding of his human possibilities are impeded. Paradoxically the law prevents him from fulfilling the commandment of the hour. Because his hand is withered he is unable to help his neighbor; his hands are tied. He can only hold out his hand to and support a fellow human being after his disability has been healed.

Jesus shows how this man can be helped. "Is it lawful on the sabbath to do good or to do harm, to save life or to kill?" Every helpful deed serves life. Every failure to help hinders life. The highest criterion is not the law, it is promoting life and serving man's well-being. In other words, justice stands above every law. Perhaps we really do not have to deal here with the fact that there are unjust laws, laws that conflict with human rights. We should be more concerned with the fact that even a just law can never be an end in itself; it is only justified to the extent that it serves humankind.

Of course this does not only apply to Jewish religious instructions. The Catholic concept of morals must also be constantly tested. Just look at the Church regulation on allowing divorced and re-married people to receive the sacrament, a subject that always causes heated discussion. At the moment these people are banned from confession and from *receiving* the eucharist, unless they part or have the firm intention of living together as "brother and sister", which means abstaining from sexual intercourse. Without doubt we are talking about a just law; according to the Church a second marriage entered into through civil law represents a serious moral transgression if the vows of the first marriage are still valid. On the other hand, however good their intentions, many people in this predicament have no chance of leading a life corresponding to the Church's concepts, based on the will of Christ. And their reasons are often very serious indeed.

In the face of this dilemma the Synod of Bishops in the Federal Republic of Germany (1975) found itself incapable of coming to a decision that could have supplied a new approach to the current rules.[3]

In 1974, in a document that was a farewell to their Bishop, the Synod of the Diocese of Basle took a different attitude.[4] The Synod did not question the indissolubility of marriage. But it wanted to help those affected to a "responsible decision of conscience". It is worth reading the following text.

The will to reform demands that every Christian and every divorced person who has re-married do what they can, here and now. The radical demands of Jesus include the readiness to have complete fidelity in marriage. But there are cases where the annulment of a second relationship would be totally irresponsible because of the deep harm it could cause to the partners and their children. Divorced people who have remarried and find themselves in such conflict may be able to test their conscience and their readiness to reform by considering the following criteria, if they wish to take part in the sacramental life of the Church:

Are they prepared to submit their guilt to God's forgiveness, and, as far as they can, take responsibility for the first partner and the children from this first marriage?

If the new relationship has been recognized by civil law, are they prepared to remain faithful to the new partner, and bring up the children according to Christian principles?

Is the desire to receive the sacraments in accordance with true Christian motives?

Does receiving the sacraments in public disturb other members of the parish and confuse them in their faith?

For Christians, honest repentance is never a private thing, but always involves responsibility towards the community of the Church and her task of dispensing forgiveness. In a subject of such importance for both those directly affected and for the community, re-married people are requested to consult a priest for a responsible decision of conscience. The priest should hold to the present pastoral guidelines.

Not all questions about re-married people receiving the sacrament have been theologically answered. But it is quite clear that Jesus demands absolute fidelity in marriage, and this remains valid. But it is also clear that Jesus is merciful to all those who have fallen short of his demands but try most sincerely to reform in every possible way. We are all dependent on God's mercy, and at the same time we are bidden in a spirit of mutual forgiveness to practice mercy towards each other, to respect the individual's decisions of conscience, and leave the final judgement to God. This attitude will lead the community to show understanding and pastoral help towards divorced people who have re-married.

The bishops of the Upper Rhine Province, Oskar Saier, Karl Lehmann and Walter Kasper, were unanimously in agreement with these statements, and on July 10 1993, they expressed this in a pastoral letter, that was very well received

("Towards pastoral aid for people from broken marriages, the divorced, and those who have re-married. Introduction, pastoral letter and principles"). In this the three Bishops express great human sensitivity and pastoral responsibility. In contrast, the reaction of the Roman Congregation of Faith seems all the more unfriendly ("The receiving of Communion by the faithful who have divorced and re-married" of September 14 1994). This document prohibits all re-married divorced persons, without exception, from receiving communion, *regardless of their situations at the time*. The three Bishops are in agreement with the Roman Congregation of Faith that the Church cannot grant divorced persons who have re-married any *official authorization* to take communion. But, in contrast to the Roman document, the Bishops allow those affected to *come towards* the table of the Lord, if they are convinced that they can take responsibility for this act after a serious *examination of conscience*. The Basle Diocesan Synod have already formulated the criteria that must be considered in the case of such self-examination.

While the document of the Congregation of Faith is permeated with the Church's thinking on legality, the statement of the Upper Rhine bishops breathes the true spirit of Jesus. Actually the Bishops' pastoral letter does not rock the foundations of the Church's teaching on marriage. It proceeds from the assumption that it is not realistic to apply the moral norm to situations that go beyond what is humanly possible. And, most important of all, in cases of doubt the well-being of people forms the final criterion, not the literal interpretation of the law.

But does this not imply that the door is open to every arbitrary act? If we ask this question we tend towards complicity with the Pharisees' fear of the law. Jesus does not give his followers a free hand so that they can act according to their *discretion*. He points towards *conscience*.

100

If we call upon our consciences after deep reflection and inward conviction, we are certainly not doing this to make our lives more pleasant, but in the knowledge that we have to become aware of our responsibilities. This often involves painful uncertainty. Obeying conscience does not mean taking the easy way out - it probably involves facing difficulties that conflict with our behavior.

And here we end up with the Pharisees again, whose thought is just as understandable as it is wrong. The more we adopt an opinion shared by others, the more certain we feel. Our own convictions are put to the test if they are not shared by others. We are afraid; is the way we have chosen the right one? This fear plagues us because we repress other opinions, yet at the same time try to push through our own ideas - only too often with violence.

In the story of the healing of the man with the withered hand it is not the law that hinders a human response but, as the text expressly says, the hardening of the heart which happens when people consider only their own views valid, *fix them to the letter of the law*, and are not prepared to examine them. Law becomes ideology. And if we do not want to suffer serious damage to the soul, we must avoid a religion that can only exist with the help of ideology.

The story of the man with the withered hand - unlike many other miracle stories - does not end with a neat conclusion. This is left to the evangelist. Obviously he is not primarily concerned with bringing his readers to the faith; instead he wants to encourage them to act from this faith, even if they end up in conflict with the law. Remember what the Lord has told us: "the sabbath was made for man, not man for the sabbath" (Mk 2,27).

3
"You give them something to eat"

The Feeding of the Five Thousand (Mk 6,30-44)

The earliest version of this story is in Mark's gospel. The other evangelists took it from him.

The apostles returned to Jesus [after they had been sent out to preach the message of repentance, Mk 6,6-13] and told him all that they had done and taught. And he said to them, "Come away by yourselves to a lonely place, and rest a while". For many were coming and going, and they had no leisure even to eat. And they went away in the boat to a lonely place by themselves. Now many saw them going, and knew them, and they ran there on foot from all the towns, and got there ahead of them. As he went ashore he saw a great throng, and he had compassion on them, because they were like sheep without a shepherd; and he began to teach them many things. And when it grew late, his disciples came to him and said, "This is a lonely place, and the hour is now very late, send them away, to go into the country and villages round about, and buy themselves something to eat." But he answered them, "You give them something to eat". And they said to him, "Shall we go and buy two hundred denarii worth of bread, and give it to them to eat?" And he said to them, "How many loaves have you? Go and see." And when they had found out, they said, "Five, and two fish." Then he commanded them all to sit down by companies upon the green grass. So they sat down in groups, by hundreds and by fifties.

And taking the five loaves and the two fish he looked up to heaven, and blessed, and broke the loaves, and gave them to the disciples to set before the people; and he divided the two fish among them all. And they all ate and were satisfied. And they took up twelve baskets full of broken pieces and of the fish. And those who ate the loaves were five thousand men. (Mk 6,30-44; Mt 14,13-21; Lk 9,10-17; Jn 6,1-13).

This story would not have surprised its first listeners because they already knew of similar occurrences in the Hebrew Bible.

Parallels in the Hebrew Bible

The Book of Exodus tells us that Yahweh fed his people with manna and quail in the desert (Ex 16). The Prayer Book of Israel and the Psalms (105,40; compare 78,24) also mention this miraculous intervention. And almost all Jews knew Elijah's story of the miracle of the meal and the oil. At the time of a great drought the prophet goes to the seaport of Zarephath, about 180 kilometers north of Jerusalem. He meets a widow before the town gate and asks her for a little bread. But she has only a handful of meal and a little oil. She is going to cook something for her son and herself, and then they will prepare for death. Calling on the name of God, the prophet assures her: "The jar of meal shall not be spent, and the jug of oil shall not fail until the day that the Lord sends rain upon the earth" (1 Kings 17,14). Of course Elijah's prophecy comes true.

Another miracle is told of Elijah's disciple and successor Elisha. Once more it is a widow who has fallen upon hard times, and is threatened by her creditors. She has nothing left but a jar of oil. The prophet tells her to borrow empty vessels from all her neighbors so that she can fill these with

103

the oil that starts to flow from her own jar (2 Kings 4,1-7). The Hebrew Bible also tells us of Elisha's miracle involving bread.

A man came from Baalshalishah, bringing the man of God bread of the first fruits, twenty loaves of barley, and fresh ears of grain in his sack. And Elisha said "Give to the men, that they may eat". But his servant said, "How am I to set this before a hundred men?" So he repeated, "Give them to the men that they may eat, for thus says the Lord, 'They shall eat and have some left'." So he set it before them. And they ate, and had some left, according to the word of the Lord (2 Kings 4,42-44).

The similarities between this and Mark's story are so striking that there is surely a connection. But while Elisha feeds a hundred men with twenty loaves of barley, Jesus only has five loaves and two fishes to feed five thousand. Even people unfamiliar with the Bible will be able to understand this message: Jesus is greater that Elisha! Could it be that Mark wants to outdo the Old Testament? However, he is not simply transferring an older story onto Jesus, although the pattern may be the same. If we read the text carefully, we come upon little details that are not unimportant towards an adequate understanding of the whole.

Firstly, people obviously put down tools and leave everything in order to hear Jesus. They spare no effort, no path is too long. They do not follow him, but hurry along ahead of him to a "lonely place." It is irrelevant to ask how they get there before him, when he is going by boat. Mark only wants to show us what extraordinary expectation these people have of Jesus. They possess what the Prophet Amos once called "...not a famine of bread, not a thirst for water, but of hearing the words of the Lord" (Amos 8,11). It is not by chance that the evangelist places Jesus and the crowd in a lonely place while Jesus instructs them. We are reminded of the people of Israel in the desert. There are no more paths following a known direction, nor leading to a particular goal. Everyone has to *search* for his or her own way. And suddenly we find that we have lost our sense of orientation.

Most of us have to face this painful experience sometime. Life seems to be moving along an even track, and then we are unexpectedly thrown off it, and left entirely to ourselves. We do not know if we are coming or going.

A woman is deserted by her husband or partner. They have lived together for years, and she trusts him completely. She has never for a moment thought that their relationship could go wrong. She is totally unprepared for what has just happened. Fury and pain, feelings of hate and revenge, despair, grief, depression and apathy overwhelm her. She is quite unable to understand this terrible thing or to tell other people about it. She hopes that he will come back, that the break will not be final. And worst of all the burning question "why?" leads to inertia during the day and sleeplessness at night. Added to all this suffering there is a loss of identity and self-esteem, and a feeling of inferiority she has never experienced before. What can she do? Throw herself out of the window, escape from herself in a new adventure with constant thoughts of him on her mind? Pray to God; what is the point? Should she go away for a couple of weeks - but where? Should she accept her fate, but would that change anything?

In this type of situation we need someone who knows how to listen. The suffering is not lessened, but we are better able to endure it. Questions cannot be answered, but we learn how to cope with them. The painful experience will not become clearer, but we can mature from it and integrate it into our lives.

The same thing is true of spiritual crises. They can overwhelm us unexpectedly, perhaps when we realize that the spirituality or pieties we have practiced over the years have suddenly become mere formalities, or that ideals treasured from our youth bear no reference to what we face today.

People who are no longer supported by anything look for a hold, not just onto *something,* but *someone.* This is true of those hurrying ahead of Jesus to the lonely place where he hopes to rest with his apostles. Jesus does not want to disappoint them "..and he had compassion on them because they were like sheep without a shepherd."

Mark takes this image from the Hebrew Bible (Num 27,17; 1 Kings 22,17). He is not thinking about individual failings or faults, but about the people who come to Jesus, looking for someone to point the way, so that their lives can have content, purpose and aim again. At the same time Mark makes it clear that this aim can only be realized if they will stop pursuing their own selfish paths, and are prepared to integrate their individual experiences into the path God reveals to them.

The words about the sheep without a shepherd revive images from the first verse of Psalm 23: "The Lord (Yahweh) is my shepherd, I shall not want; he makes me lie down *in green pastures* "(Ps 23,1f). So that the slower ones among us can understand the allusion, the evangelist expressly mentions that Jesus invites the people to sit down *"upon the green grass".* In this way he also underlines what Jesus is talking about; he wants to bring his countrymen back to their actual shepherd, to Yahweh. For he is the Lord, and "I shall not want."

But man does not live by the word of God alone; he needs his daily bread. We notice that it is the apostles who are the first to think about food. This is understandable, because they have just returned from their preaching duties, and they are exhausted (Mk 6,6-13). A missionary in Africa once told me that the mothers in his parish encouraged their children to start screaming when they felt that his sermon was too long. The twelve behave in the same way. But they would be embarrassed to interrupt his preaching by saying that peoples' stomachs are rumbling. So they find a pretext; "...the hour is now late; *send them away*, to go into the country and villages round about and buy themselves something to eat". Jesus takes the hint; the apostles want to teach him something. But he has a better idea: "*You* give them something to eat."

Jesus proclaims *eternal salvation* to us all; are the apostles called to look after our *bodily comforts*? No service to God without service to the world? Commitment to here and now as a criterion for belief in what lies beyond?

There is no doubt that all these things are part of the central core of the good tidings that Jesus proclaims, which is then passed down by his apostles. But in fact the story of the feeding of the five thousand is aimed at something totally different.

To remind us: The people follow Jesus because they are hungry for the *word of God*. Their thoughts bend only towards this. And they take the food that he gives them as naturally as they absorb his words.

The evangelists frequently point to the astonished or enthusiastic reaction of the crowd in these miracle stories. After the healing of the lame man at Capernaum Mark says "...they were all amazed and glorified God, saying 'We never saw anything like this!' " (Mk 2,12). We might well expect this kind of chorus, (absent from the Gift miracles) at the end of the episode of the feeding of the five thousand. But if we read the text carefully we can see that there would be no reason for it. There is no evidence that the people present really take much notice of what is happening. They sit on the grass, they are given a piece of bread and a little dried fish. Why should they be surprised?

The Symbolism of Numbers

Mark does not intend to emphasize Jesus's power and greatness by telling us of his miracles. His readers would have immediately understood the little hint about Jesus outdoing Elisha! Elisha feeds a hundred men with twenty loaves of bread, Jesus five thousand with only five. In contrast to John (Jn 6), Mark does not allude to the Last Supper.

We realize Mark's intentions when we become aware of the symbolism of numbers. Why precisely five loaves, two fish, twelve baskets? In this short episode Mark twice mentions that the apostles have a supply of five loaves and two fishes, which add up to seven. From time immemorial the people of Israel had regarded number seven as sacred, a symbol of God so to speak. Obviously the evangelist is reminding his readers that first of all man must nourish himself with the food that has come down from heaven and *gives him eternal life.* John further expands this thought in his gospel (Jn 6,33-58). Man does not live from bread alone, but from "everything that proceeds out of the mouth of the Lord" (Deut 8,3). This is written in the Hebrew Bible, *and* in Matthew and Luke (Mt 4,4; Lk 4,4). And when Jesus raises his eyes towards heaven at the beginning of the meal, he is not doing it to ask God for a miracle, he is saying a prayer of praise and thanks - or grace as we would call it today.

But we have not completely deciphered the basic symbolism behind the miracle. According to Jewish understanding at the time, the Word of God was found in three groups of biblical texts: the *Torah* (the five books of Moses) the Books of the *Prophets*, and the remaining *manuscripts* (Psalms, Lamentations, Wisdom and History).

We have good reason to believe that the five loaves of bread point to the five books of Moses. We also have evidence from the first century that the rabbis compared the Torah with bread, which was the staple food at that time. The two fishes symbolize the two other texts, the Books of the Prophets and the collection of manuscripts.[1] *These* are fed to the people present, and Jesus gives them to all those who turn to him.

Even though the supply of bread and fish is so scant it does not decrease! Twelve baskets are left over from it. Like seven, twelve is also a sacred number for the Jews; an expression of the *fullness* of God. The supply of food that Jesus offers - the Word of God - is inexhaustible. The whole of humankind can be filled with it. The knowledge that the story of the feeding of the five thousand is so rich in symbolism helps us towards an appropriate understanding: only when we allow ourselves to be led by God's Word and Wisdom do we find the way to a fulfilled life. But there is another important point. After the apostles realize that the people have hardly eaten anything during the day, they want to send them into the neighboring villages to buy something. Although there is no sign of a beast of burden to carry provisions for such a crowd, Jesus pretends not to hear the apostles' suggestion. In fact he tells them rather provocatively, "*You* give them something to eat!"

This is their *task*. What the apostles give the people is not bread, as we have seen, but God's Word that gives life - and the people cannot *buy* this for themselves. They can only receive it thankfully from those who also have nothing in their hands and are aware of it.

The French novelist Georges Bernanos (1888-1948) writes

about this theme with considerable theological depth in his novel "The Diary of a Country Priest." As the title suggests, this book is the diary of an inexperienced and sickly young priest who works in a forlorn and remote village in Flanders.[2] His parish is "bored stiff", so he decides on a bold but hopeless attempt to uncover the stupidity of conventional piety, and expose the contradiction between the institution of the Church, that anyway functions as the dogsbody to the secular powers, and real Christianity, which the Church professes to represent. Of course this simple priest knows how his colleagues judge him; for example the good-natured priest in the neighboring village of Torcy:

"You're a queer specimen! I shouldn't think there's another softy like you in the whole diocese! And you work like a cart-horse, sweating your guts out...Really His Grace must have been very hard up for priests to have given you the handling of a parish. Luckily the parish is solid enough - or you might break it.

The young priest does not need to be told this:

By nature I'm probably coarse-grained, for I confess that I have always been repelled by the "lettered" priest. After all, to cultivate clever people is merely a way of dining out, and a priest has no right to go out to dinner in a world full of starving people...I am no longer fit to guide a parish. I have neither prudence, nor judgement, nor common sense, nor real humility.

Which means that he is the wrong man in the wrong place. It is a plain statement, and we do not have the impression that this priest is waiting for someone to contradict it. There is also no sign of his approval of his own humility - when this happens, humility can change in a flash to pride in a modesty worn only on one's sleeve. But here there is someone who has come to terms with himself as a "useless fellow". It is both magnificent and moving that he never despairs.

Our Lord had need of a witness, and I was chosen, doubtless for lack of anyone better, as one calls in a passer-by. I should be crazy indeed to imagine that I had a part, a real part in it. Already it is too much that God should have given me the grace to be present when a soul became reconciled to hope again—those solemn nuptials!

These spontaneous sentences describe the priest's last meeting with a countess who lives near the village. She is disgusted by her husband's love affairs, she has to bear with her daughter's hatred of her, and yet suffers more than anything from the pain caused her by the death of her eighteen-month-old son many years ago. Her whole raison d'etre is the love she has for this dead child. And now the wall of pride and arrogance she has barricaded herself behind for half a lifetime is torn down by the clumsiness of this simple and uneducated priest. Naive and child-like, he is the only person who enables her to renounce her feigned superciliousness, so that she can find inner stillness, and make peace with God.

The countess is found dead in her bed the day after this crucial meeting, but this is not just a literary trick. Perhaps there really are moments when we believe that we must die of happiness? Before the countess goes to sleep that night, she writes the priest a letter.

Monsieur le Curé, I don't suppose you can imagine my state of mind when you left me, since all such questions of

psychology probably mean nothing at all to you. What can I say to you? I have lived in the most horrible solitude, alone with the desperate memory of a child. And it seems to me that another child has brought me to life again. I hope you won't be annoyed with me for regarding you as a child. Because you are! May God keep you one for ever!
I wonder what you've done to me. How did you manage it? Or rather, I no longer ask myself. All's well. I didn't think one could ever possibly be resigned. And really this isn't resignation! There is no resignation in me, and there I wasn't wrong in my presentiment. I'm not resigned, I'm happy. I don't want anything.

How does such a change of heart take place? The country priest does not think it is his doing: "I am nothing more than a poor priest, very unworthy and very wretched...". But he trusts in Jesus's words "*You* give them something to eat!"

To Fulfill Jesus's Mission

"*You* give them something to eat!" This command is a massive criticism of some people in office who forget that they themselves have nothing to say. All they have to do is pass on what they have previously received from Jesus's hands. They are the legates, representatives, and *in this sense,* authorized to practice a power that they are not entitled to practice in their own names. "Unfortunately there have always been people in office, legates of Jesus who carry their mission, their authority, their power of attorney like a monstrance in front of them. But Christ alone belongs in the monstrance."[3]

There is always the danger that people in office represent nobody but themselves. Instead of simply fulfilling Jesus's mission, they inflate their own authority, something irreconcilable with the gospel proclaimed by Jesus. It is enough to mention all the honorary titles and ranks that still command high esteem in certain Church circles. Apart from the venerables, the reverends, and the most reverends, there are the most reverend excellencies, and the equally most reverend eminences, and reigning over them all is His Holiness. Of course members of this male hierarchy know how to address each other correctly. But according to Jesus, authority is based on the kingdom of God, and not on the assumption of an exalted title; it lies in the merciful and humble performance of his mission *"You* give them something to eat".

This command is the high point of the feeding of the five thousand. Naturally the evangelist had his readers in mind, especially those who were called to spread the faith. But his statement has a timeless validity. Anyone with a special position in the Church can be tempted to defend it jealously, to insist on his own authority, and to forget that every "special position" is responsible for rendering a particular service to the community of the faithful. And the "simple faithful" will always tend to shift the burden of proclaiming the faith onto people in office.

The miracle of the feeding of the five thousand happens over and over again, whenever those in office fulfill their mission faithfully, without looking over their shoulders for recognition and reward. It happens whenever they serve the poor before the secure, whenever they refuse to be served as Princes of the Church and discharge their duties to the community of the faithful, aware that they are nothing more than "useless fellows". The same miracle also happens when individual believers stop excusing themselves from the action because their abilities and strengths are limited, and involve themselves in spreading the kingdom of God. This means first and foremost working for the good of others, for justice, peace, and the protection of creation.

And so the discrepancy between our individual limitations and what we are aiming at no longer carries much weight. We can then believe that new forces will be freed and the seed will germinate, bearing fruit thirtyfold, fortyfold, even a hundredfold (Mk 4,8), so that much will come of little. The little that the apostles put into Jesus's hands, and then receive again from his hands, is surely enough *if they will only hand it on.*

This is what Georges Bernanos illustrates in the character of the country priest. If we find this story edifying yet bearing no resemblance to reality, we should remind ourselves of the life of a poor simple priest, who compared himself to the usual cleric as "a poor village idiot."[4] His name was Jean-Baptiste Marie Vianney (1786-1859) the Curé of Ars, who was canonized by Pope Pius XI in 1929. His eighty-five sketches for sermons have survived him. They are laboriously worked extracts from books of sermons which served clerics as models at the time. Like Bernanos's country priest, Vianney suffered from human shortcomings and theological ignorance. And yet he managed to transform a god-forsaken hamlet into a model parish, although a predecessor had said that the inhabitants could only be distinguished from the animals because they had been baptized.

He was anything but an outstanding preacher; he did not move people by finely crafted sermons, but opened their hearts to God by bearing eloquent witness to Him.

Jean-Baptiste Marie Vianney was simply a poor country priest who had nothing to counteract his boundless lack of education and knowledge except his boundless trust in God. This enabled him to approach his fellow human beings with open arms.

We are reminded of Paul; "..behold we live... as poor, but making many rich; as having nothing, and yet possessing everything" (2 Cor 6,10). Paul is not referring to his own experiences but to the situation of the faithful, who are torn lifelong between the wish for sanctity and the tendency to sin. It is not trust in ourselves but an unshakable trust in God's help that makes us realize that Jesus's demands are not excessive.

Lothar Zenetti expresses this in a poem alluding to Paul's words and to the Jewish-Christian history of salvation:[5]

We have so many fears
but look - we live

Those who believe in you
go through deserts
find manna and water in the rocks

Those who believe in you
go through water
with dry feet through raging rivers

Those who believe in you
go through walls
as in a dream through closed doors

Those who believe in you
go through flames
living torches that yet do not burn

Those who believe in you
go through the darkness
seem to die and look they live

We have so many fears
but look we live

What can prevent us from giving others to eat when God puts himself into our empty hands, if we will only keep them open for him?

4
Of Devils, Demons and Evil Spirits

The Gerasene Demoniac (Mk 5,1-20)

The meaning of some stories in the gospels is so clear because we recognize ourselves in them. There is the parable of the Prodigal Son (Lk 15,11-32), which is actually about the father's goodness, or the episode of Jesus's meeting with "the woman of the city who was a sinner". She weeps tears over his feet, and then, comforted, leaves in the certitude that God's mercy is infinitely greater than all human failure (Lk 7,36-50).

Some of the other stories demand rather more from us and are difficult to understand. The miracle of the healing of the Gerasene Demoniac belongs to this disconcerting category.

They came to the other side of the sea, to the country of the Gerasenes. And when he had come out of the boat, there met him a man with an unclean spirit, who lived among the tombs; and no one could bind him any more, even with a chain; for he had often been bound with fetters and chains, but the chains he wrenched apart, and the fetters he broke in pieces; and no one had the strength to subdue him. Night and day among the tombs and on the mountains he was always crying out, and bruising himself with stones. And when he saw Jesus from afar, he ran and worshipped him; and crying out with a loud voice he said "What have you to do with me, Jesus, Son of the Most High God? I adjure you by God, do not torment me." For he had said to him, "Come

117

out of the man, you unclean spirit!" And Jesus asked him, "What is your name?" He replied "My name is legion; for we are many." And he begged him eagerly not to send them out of the country. Now a great herd of swine was feeding there on the hillside; and they begged him, "Send us to the swine, let us enter them." So he gave them leave. And the unclean spirits came out, and entered the swine; and the herd, numbering about two thousand, rushed down the steep bank into the sea, and were drowned in the sea.

The herdsmen fled, and told it in the city and in the country. And people came to see what it was that had happened. And they came to Jesus, and saw the demoniac sitting there, clothed and in his right mind; the man who had had the legion; and they were afraid. And those who had seen it told what had happened to the demoniac and to the swine. And they began to beg Jesus to depart from their neighborhood. And as he was getting into the boat, the man who had been possessed with demons begged him that he might be with him. But he refused, and said to him, "Go home to your friends, and tell them how much the Lord has done for you." And he went away, and began to claim in the Decapolis how much Jesus had done for him; and all men marvelled (Mk 5,1-20; compare Mt 8,28-34; Lk 8,26-39).

An Offensive Story?

Over the years scholars have been uneasy about this episode. In his "Life of Jesus", first published in 1835, the Protestant theologian David Friedrich Strauss ridiculed the story about the devils entering the swine; "even interpreters of the Bible with strong faith run out of credulity." Another Protestant scholar, Hermann Gunkel (1862-1932) said that it sounded "like a fairy story that is not without humor, but certainly has nothing to do with the historical Jesus". Rudolf Bultmann, one of the founders of modern Bible studies, has no doubt that "here a popular comic tale has been transferred to Jesus" in which the widespread motif of the "devil deceived" plays a part. In his book "Why I Am Not a Christian" Bertrand Russell, the English philosopher, mathematician and sociologist thinks that it "was not very nice" of Jesus to loose the devils into the swine.[1]

Therefore it is not surprising that Christians without any theological training find this story rather bizarre and tend to place it among fables or folklore. But taking literature seriously does not mean that everything must be taken at face value. We can only do justice to an author's views by analyzing the text with some care. This applies here.

A few explanations may help to clarify the scene. We are told that this story happens in the area of the Decapolis, more exactly, in the country of the Gerasenes. At that time the Decapolis (the land of ten cities) was largely gentile. It lay east of the Jordan between the Dead Sea and the Sea of Galilee. One of the most important towns in the Decapolis was Gerasa (today Dsherash), and it is here that the event took place. But the naming of this town is a problem. Gerasa was about 55 kilometers southwest of the Sea of Galilee. There is no other lake near it into which the swine could have hurled themselves.

According to Matthew the whole event - in a slightly altered form - happens near the little town of Gadara (Mt 8,28-34). Some of the old manuscripts of Mark's gospel adopt this version, but this also presents problems, as Gadara is to the southeast, a good ten kilometers from the sea of Galilee. Yet another version can probably be attributed to Origen (c.185-253/4), who places the event in Gergesa, which lies on the east bank of the Sea of Galilee. It also commends itself because there is a steep cliff down to the sea about two kilometers away from the town, although people have searched in vain for the tombs mentioned in the text. Remains of this town can still be seen in the ruins of Kurse.[2]

These later suggestions seem to indicate that in all probability the *original* story took place in Gerasa. If this is the case, we may be dealing with the work of someone who did not know the area, had only heard of the Decapolis and the famous Gerasa, and was unable to locate them exactly. He would have had no idea what a long journey he was putting the swine through because of his ignorance of geography.

So the doubtful situation of the town is at least a hint that the story is not a homogenous whole in this form. If it originally did not even happen near the sea, but was later put there by someone (the evangelist?) in ignorance of the area, it would mean that the drowning of the swine was not part of the original story material, but was slotted in later as an afterthought. It is striking that nowhere else in the gospels is the fate of demons being driven out described with such relish. That the detailed description ("Legion", "numbering about two thousand") must have made quite an impression on readers of the time is shown by a comparison with Matthew's version. We know he based it on Mark. Similar to the healing of the blind near Jericho, (compare Mk 10,46-52; Mt 20,29-34) Matthew doubles the number of those healed in order to underline Jesus's effective power. According to him there are suddenly *two* men who have to be freed from the demons (Mt 8,28). But as far as these evil spirits are concerned, Matthew cuts the text radically; he neither mentions their name nor a specific number. Obviously he is already having some reservations.

All these inconsistencies suggest that the story has gone through various stages. Whether the episode of the swine was put in later or belonged to the original text is a question that really cannot be answered. Even if we assume it was there from the beginning it does not necessarily mean that it reflects any historical fact. But we can be sure that *Jesus was active as a successful exorcist,* although it is hard to say *which descriptions referring to this attribute* have an historical core. As far as our text is concerned, it seems that Joachim Gnilka, the bible scholar from Munich, has hit the nail on the head when he writes "it is highly probable that there is no concrete historical memory because of the symbolic content".[3] Walter Schmithals, another scholar, is even more unequivocal when he speaks of a "theological poem" shaped with "particular care".[4]

Satan's Fringe Existence

Many people cannot take the demons in the Bible seriously. But we have to ask whether *all that is implied in belief in them* is really out of date. The fact that Jesus and his contemporaries viewed the world quite differently from us does not mean that we can dismiss their view as meaningless.

The sceptics among us may question the existence of evil spirits, demons and devils but the biblical authors took these for granted. It was as natural for Jesus and his fellow countrymen to believe that dark forces walked abroad as to believe that the sun turned round the earth. Although part of his proclamation, these assumptions in themselves are not an essential or binding part of our belief in him. Today many of us may well ask whether we cannot simply dispense with devils and demons, although belief in them was widespread in the ancient world.

But if we study the Bible rather more carefully, we notice that the earliest sections (ten centuries before Christ) speak neither of good nor of evil spirits. There was no need of mediators between God and man. The Yahweh God turned directly to Abraham or Moses. In later centuries when people perceived God as distant, angels (Greek: *ángelos* meaning messenger) stepped in to fill the enormous void between him and man. This development led to a conception of evil as a personified force. The oldest answer to this question in the Bible is expressed in the account of the Fall from Paradise (Gen 3). This emphasizes that evil does not stem from God - man is blamed for it. Most readers of the Bible tend to identify the serpent with the devil. But this view would have been completely foreign to the story teller; for him the serpent is merely a symbol of a sinister force, subject to God's will.

In the end *everything* leads back to God and nothing can happen against his will. This is testified in the extremely old statement (the tenth or ninth century before Christ) according to which *God himself* in his "anger...incited" David to hold a census (2 Sam 24,1). At the time this was regarded as "godless" because Yahweh alone was Lord of his people. About 300 B.C. a later biblical writer returned to the same subject, although this time the initiator was not God but the devil: "*Satan* stood up against Israel, and incited David to number Israel" (1 Chron 21,1).

Obviously the thought that God could incite man to evil had become intolerable. This was why people resorted to Satan, God's adversary, and made him responsible. We cannot be sure to what extent this idea was influenced by Zoroastrianism, the ancient religion of Iran, which recognized a primal principle of good and one of evil, in eternal conflict with each other. The fact is that Satan has only a fringe existence in the Hebrew Bible; there are only three references to him (Zech 3,1; Job 1,6;2,1; Chron 21,1).[5]

The same is true of Jesus's proclamation. In almost all places where the synoptic gospels speak of Satan, they do not reflect Jesus's preaching, but the catechetical instructions to the early Christian community. The only historically authentic words of Jesus which refer to Satan are found in Luke: "I saw Satan fall like lightning from heaven" (10,18). This does not say that we must be afraid of "Satan's cunning and power" (lines from a well known hymn) but rather that he has actually played out his role because Jesus's message has liberated us.[6]

We know that Jesus locates the real cause of evil in the world in the failure of *love*, which can help and heal those enmeshed in evil - it has nothing to do with Satan's work. This is what he demonstrates so obviously when he casts out demons. Perhaps it would not be superficial to say that this is not simply driving out the *devil*, because the evangelists make an exact distinction between *the devil* or *Satan* as individuals and the *demons* that so often appear in their versions of the gospels.

In Judaism demons were also described as *unclean spirits*. This has to do with the Jewish conception of cleanliness at the time. You were made unclean by coming into contact with certain people, animals, objects or districts. In order to take part in services again, you had to undergo certain rites of cleanliness. Gentiles, and also workers who plied an unworthy trade, were considered unclean, for example, grave diggers, tanners, traders. Swine were regarded as particularly unclean. Graves and cemeteries were also unclean places. People assumed that demons liked living in graveyards, hence the term "unclean spirits".

The demons mentioned in the gospels *should not be identified with Satan*; they are an independent phenomenon. In fact in the ancient world, every unfamiliar illness was attributed to the workings of a demonic power. This view was widespread in the Middle Ages, and survived to the time of Humanism.[7] So from our modern point of view, it is quite in order for us to interpret Jesus's exorcism as *healing the sick* in the broadest sense.

Jesus also had numerous contemporaries in Palestine who were highly successful as exorcists, and we know this from Jesus himself - the words were not put into his mouth by the evangelists: "And if I cast out demons by Beelzebul (a Canaan deity, "Baal the Prince") by whom do your sons cast them out?" (Mt 12,27).

What have you to do with me?

The man living in the tombs of Gerasa seems to have been a particularly difficult case of possession. From all accounts he was in a state of raging mania. Even chains could not bind him. We are told that he was possessed of an unclean spirit, whose name was "Legion". This meant that the spirit had the strength of a whole host of demons, and the man was extremely dangerous.

And yet it seems from the first moment that there was a fear of great darkness behind his screams and rages: "What have you to do with me, Jesus, Son of the Most High God? I adjure you by God, do not torment me."

This declaration of faith in Jesus can be traced back to the narrator of the story; he is actually giving us the key to the whole episode. Faced by the power of Jesus, the man begins to tremble. He is so powerless that he adjures Jesus by the name of God. "What have you to do with me, Jesus Son of God?" He means this literally. "We live in different worlds. I never had anything to do with you, and I never will. We are separated for eternity". These are the words of a sinner, a god-less man. And *he* embodies the possessed. When a man turns away from God he becomes his own lord and master. But at the same time he loses his hold on everything and his sense of orientation. He has strayed far from the path.

Naturally the evangelist is not thinking of a modern atheist, who for one reason or another is convinced that there is no God, but still tries to lead his life according to his conscience, respects human rights, and practices love for his neighbor. He means the person who knows very well that there *is* a God, but does not care. Like the demoniac who does not deny God ("I adjure you by God") the practicing atheist can recite his creed - perhaps every Sunday in church - and yet lead a godless life.

Of course I do not mean that a godless person is by nature a sinner, a cut-throat or a monster. In fact the demoniac in the story is not hurting anyone else. He strikes himself with stones and tears off his own clothes. In describing this the evangelist exposes the nature of sin. Most believers think that sin mainly exists in violating the commandments or disregarding laws and in the human aberrations linked to these. But this is a very superficial way of thinking, and the story gives an entirely different point of view. Sins are not individual violations of specific, precisely stipulated moral norms (such violations are a result of sin). Sin consists primarily in either an open or a hidden rejection of God. Such a person takes his life in his own hands. He wants to come to terms with his past by himself; to shape the present alone, plan his future alone. So he relies entirely upon his own performance, his own strength, his own ability. He does not like to receive anything or to be obliged to anyone else, and strives for only one thing—his autonomy. He sees himself as his own redeemer. He is entirely of one mind with the demoniac who hurls himself towards Jesus: "What have you to do with me, Jesus, Son of the Most High God?"

In one of his most moving parables, the Prodigal Son (Lk 15,11-32) Jesus illustrates how a person can fall victim to demonic powers if he lives his life apart from God. What causes the son to rebel? Why does he want to leave home at all costs, when he obviously lacks nothing? The story seems to imply that he feels his ties to the parental home as shackles. He has had enough of good advice being poured out with every spoonful of soup. He longs for "life". He longs to taste freedom and shape his existence according to his own ideas. He desires his liberty, but he confuses it with caprice. But when he reaches rock bottom he begins to understand that freedom does not consist in a lack of commitment; it is only possible within a special form of commitment. The son only possesses all the rights of a son in his father's house. In foreign parts he is deemed a foreigner, and is caught up in ever new dependencies. This commitment to the father (that is, to God) is imperative, if a person is not to fall victim to the tawdry and second rate, usually to some kind of ideology that he then turns into an idol. Only acknowledgement of the definitive authority of a higher power makes a person free in this world. Expressing this in religious terms means that we have to refer to our consciences (through which we hear the voice of God) when we are faced with social pressures, state laws and church regulations. Only then can we say freely and with confidence: Here I stand. I can no other.

We can realize our freedom within a commitment that, of necessity, has to be transcendental. Accordingly God is the ground that makes it possible for us to do this. For God alone can protect us from being dependent on this world.

A Demoniac Figure in Literature

Dostoevski illustrates this in his novel "The Possessed",[8] which is also an updated version of the story of the Gerasene demoniac. Dostoevski quotes this at the beginning of his book.

The work was based on an event that shook all Russia at the time. In November 21 1869 near Moscow a revolutionary group murdered a former member because he had withdrawn from the circle. In this crime Dostoevski saw the logical consequences of the atheistic and nihilistic tendencies that were attracting disciples among the intellectuals of his time.

The novel is about a group of people whose thought is so poisoned that everything they do is destructive. The root of this attitude is their negation of God, which inevitably leads to despising mankind.

All the strands of the plot are knotted together in the character of the criminal Nikolay Stavrogin, who experiments with people as a researcher experiments with mice. Talented and spoilt from early youth, this young man is less the product than the exponent of a subversive and ruinous society, senseless and bored, with crime as its only gratification. In his "Confession", Stavrogin admits that his life bores him to death. (Dostoevski's Russian publisher found this document so scandalous that he refused to print it). Stavrogin also confesses that he has raped his landlady's thirteen-year-old daughter. Soon afterwards she takes her own life. A few days before this he had watched her mother beating her savagely for a theft she had not committed. There is no more terrible scene in all Dostoevski's works as when the child, who has been raped, raises her small fist towards her torturer before she goes down from the house to a wooden shack to hang herself. Stavrogin *knows* that her deep sense of shame will lead her to kill herself, but he does nothing to stop her. He just observes every step, every movement of the despairing girl from his window, and then he actually follows her until she reaches the shack. In his confession afterwards he describes every detail: "At the moment when I raised myself on tiptoe, it came to me that when I had been watching a red spider as I sat lost in thought by the window, I had imagined to myself how I would stand on tiptoe and press my eye to this crack".

Neither uncontrolled passion nor pathological sexuality play a part in this foul deed. What actually happens goes beyond the bounds of our comprehension; we are overcome by pure horror. Stavrogin does not calculate, his actions are totally unmotivated. He himself does not know why he has done this terrible thing. He does not once *ask* himself the reason for his criminal actions. In his opinion there is no such thing as crime. His doings are only shameful and criminal according to others. The fury that overwhelms him after his deed has nothing to do with himself or his victim, it is only that he has a momentary fear of discovery and punishment. As a result he determines to ruin his life somehow and as repulsively as possible. For this reason he decides to marry a crippled simple-minded girl "just to see what will come of it".

Once as my eyes fell on the cripple Marya Timoyevna Lebyadkin who served in all the low taverns - at that time she was not quite mad, but only an exalted idiot and secretly madly in love with me - I suddenly decided to marry her. The thought of a union between a Stavrogin and this lowest of all creatures made my nerves shudder. I couldn't imagine anything more crass.

It is significant that Stavrogin never speaks about guilt in his "Confession". As he does not recognize any moral law, it is no surprise that all awareness of guilt should pass him by. "I declare that I neither know nor feel good nor evil, and that I have not only lost all feeling for them, but also hold fast to the idea that there is no good, no evil." It is hardly necessary to emphasize that such detachment results in total unrelatedness, an absolute isolation from one's fellow human beings. Stavrogin is able to take this into account when he confesses that he can never love anyone.

Someone who thinks like this *creates fear*. It is no surprise that he allows a murderer, church robber and arsonist who has escaped from a lunatic asylum to dispose of his wife, her brother, and a girl who witnesses this deed by chance, so that he can give all his attention to his lover. But she leaves him after spending one night with him when he declares his love for her. "What a strange declaration!" she replies. At daybreak she suddenly knows that there are worlds between her and Stavrogin:

I have to confess that I cannot rid myself of the thought that you must have something awful, disgusting, some bloodshed on your conscience... but something that would make you look absolutely ludicrous. Save yourself from telling me, if it is true. I would laugh you to scorn. I would laugh at you for the rest of my life...

Anyone who disregards all the rules, who does not recognize ethical standards becomes a caricature of himself. This knowledge is deadly. Although Stavrogin says in his parting letter that ridicule cannot frighten him, he hangs himself. Perhaps Stavrogin is psychologically the most daring character thought up by Dostoevski. He is one of the most demon-ridden figures in all literature. He personifies perversion.

From a theological point of view, this novel illustrates the difference between freedom and capriciousness. People who see themselves as the measure of all things falsely imagine that they are free, but they "have only the freedom of the leaf that has fallen from the tree and must now obey the wind, which blows it where it wills; one of the most pernicious aspects of a demonized life is its bondage to the caprice of the moment."[9] It is easy to understand why Dostoevski's novel speaks so often of the horror that Stavrogin evokes in his ambience. This is also true of the man from Gerasa. We know only too well why his countrymen try to bind him with chains.

A Farce about the Devil Deceived?

If we read the miracle of the Demoniac from Gerasa with this background in mind, we suddenly realize that we are not dealing with an improbable or fantastic story. The warning is only too clear: if we break away from God we will fall prey to demons.

The demoniac lives in tombs, dedicated to death he "lives" among the dead; whatever he does is marked by death.

This is true of a deluded person who, in his longing for autonomy, has broken away from God, the source of all life. He destroys himself. The story expresses this when the man beats himself with stones. As long as he will have nothing to do with God he cannot be helped. But he can allow himself to be helped at any time. This is the real miracle. Jesus seems to be uninvited. To put it theologically, God's grace antici- pates man's every action and his workings. That God's care of humankind (and this is what we call *grace* in theological language) is simply far greater than any human effort is emphasized when the demoniac worships Jesus. Even *before* he resists ("What have you to do with me?"), he has been conquered.

God's power is infinitely stronger than the most powerful demon. The story clarifies this in the asking of names. In the ancient world the name of a person was not a chance attribute, but said something about the person's nature.

130

Knowing a person's name meant you had a certain power over them; remember the fairy tale of Rumpelstiltskin! The demon *has to* give his name, and this suggests his helplessness. To our astonishment we hear that a whole army of demons is forced to reveal its name. The powerlessness of the demonic facing the power of the divine could hardly be more drastically expressed.

Evil cannot exist before God. The demons reveal this by giving up their position before Jesus intervenes at all. They plead with him not to drive them out of the country. Obviously they are afraid of being banished into the desert (Tob 8,3, where a demon "fled to the remotest parts of Egypt") and of losing their place of work.[10] To put it the other way round, even when evil has no more chance, it still seeks out the weak points in man, to insure its continued existence.

Our description of the banishing of demons is in no way unique. There are similar accounts in ancient heathen literature in which wicked spirits are banished into animals. A Greek exorcism that has come down to us banishes the demons into a bull, and a Babylonian invocation proffers a pig as a new home.[11]

When Jesus allows the demons to go into the swine, the story is simply proceeding along contemporary patterns. Besides, swine were considered unclean by the Jews, and therefore despised. The self-destructive effect of evil is shown by the fact that the now greatly disturbed pigs run in the wrong direction and are all drowned in the sea, taking the demons with them.

It is deceptive to think of this story as a variation of the farce of the devil deceived. Doubtless it has elements of comedy, but it is clear that the storyteller is not so much interested in entertaining us as in putting a theological point of view. We must remind ourselves that the countryside near

Gerasa was largely inhabited by gentiles. If the evil spirits take over almost two thousand swine, and these rush into the sea, it means that Jesus has destroyed just the same number of demons. To put it clearly, wherever Jesus appears, evil spirits have no room to move. Jesus's power is boundless. It goes beyond the limits of the Jewish religion. He is the savior of all humankind.

Anyone listening to this story today might well bring up the question of damages. But that would be rather like picking holes in the first printed version of the Luther Bible by referring to the latest edition of the Oxford Concise Dictionary.

What is relevant to this story of the demoniac's healing also applies to many other biblical texts: it is not subject to the dictate of logic, but follows the law of theo-logic.

Neither the herdsmen nor the people they tell about it waste one single word on the loss of the swine. When they see the demoniac "sitting there, clothed and in his right mind" they are "afraid". This does not mean that they feel normal fear or terror. Their fear means the reverential awe that overcomes us when we are confronted with what is sacred, divine or numinous.

The story would not be complete without the two reactions to the experience. The inhabitants of Gerasa beg Jesus to leave. This is an expression of their lack of understanding. They are among those that "hear but do not understand, see but do not perceive" (Is 6,9). They do not refuse to recognize the presence and evidence of the divine. But they refuse him: "What have you to do with me?" The man who is healed is different. He asks Jesus if he may stay with him, thus expressing the will to follow him. "Go home to your friends, and tell them how much the Lord (Yahweh, God) has done for you, and how he has had mercy on you." This can be translated today as "the Christian has *nowhere else* to go but to where he lived before, but this time he is *a different person.*"[12]

From a literary point of view, the account of the Gerasene demoniac has a double ending, in that both possible reactions are shown in relation to Jesus's powerful deed. But there is a *theological* alternative and the evangelist confronts his readers with it. *In relation to ourselves,* the story is open-ended. Are we not always tempted to say with the demoniac "What have you to do with me?"

Devils and Demons - Personified Beings?

We now have to face a question that would never have bothered someone living when the story was written. Demons were imagined as personified beings and attributed with the power to intervene in man's destiny. Was this belief simply part of the world view at the time, or are we to accept these premises in Holy Scripture as still binding and valid?

We assume that there was always a link between the demonic and man. Man was either subject to its influences, or could take up arms against it. In our story the power of the demons depends on their taking possession of a *man.* They have absolutely no control over the swine, who rush with them towards the abyss and so destroy them. The demoniac is only evil to the extent that demons can take their pleasure with him. But they do not extinguish his being; they pervert it into a "sub-being". Or, to put it more clearly, he is not unavoidably evil; evil simply represents one of his possibilities. We never experience evil "in itself", but are constantly faced with cruel casts of mind, malicious attitudes and ideas that are expressions of the evil that is inherent in a *person.* Evil meets us in all those forms assumed by human misdemeanor; in defamation of character, stubborn silence, irreconcilable behavior, deviant thinking, unjust dealing and

133

reprehensible deeds. We can list them: repression, torture, cruelty, defending the strong and neglecting the weak, capricious and violent acts, humiliating and violating others, deceiving and disillusioning our credulous fellow human beings. Go through the whole list of human misdeeds and crimes, from the fatal apple on the tree in the Garden of Eden right through to the Holocaust and the genocide in our time. In simple words, we never experience evil as something independent in itself, but as something that dwells within humankind, which means *within us*.

The story of the man from Gerasa expresses this: "And when he saw Jesus... crying out with a loud voice he said: 'What have you to do with me?...do not torment *me!*'" Obviously the man's speech melts into the speech of the demon, so that both seem to become one person - yet the man cannot simply be identified with the demon. We hear this from Jesus's question which is clearly addressed to the *demon*: "Come out of the man, you unclean spirit!" And Jesus asked him, "What is your name?"

Asking whether demons actually exist or not misses the real point. To a certain extent it defuses the problem. We may then establish that the story of the demoniac from Gerasa is not about the personification of demons but about *man's tendency towards evil (evil as a possibility within him!). Also that he is evil - demonic - to the extent that he makes himself the measure of all things in his thought and action (What have you to do with me?).*

This raises a question both psychologically and theologically interesting; is the demoniac still himself, or is he "another"? After what I have already said the answer is quite complex. The demoniac does not simply have the demon in him; he *is* demonic. To put it differently; he is distanced from God and therefore a *demonic* person, but as a demonic *person* he is *himself*. Paul expresses this ambiguity in human

134

existence so clearly in a letter to the Romans:

I do not understand my own actions. For I do not what I want, but I do the very thing I hate. Now if I do what I do not want, I agree that the law is good. So then it is no longer I that do it, but sin which dwells within me. For I know that nothing good dwells within me, that is, in my flesh. I can will what is right, but I cannot do it. For I do not do the good I want, but the evil I do not want is what I do. Now if I do what I do not want, it is no longer I that do it, but sin which dwells within me. So I find it to be a law that when I want to do right, evil lies close at hand. For I delight in the law of God, in my inmost self, but I see in my members another law at war with the law of my mind and making me captive to the law of sin which dwells in my members. Wretched man that I am! Who will deliver me from this body of death? (Rom 7,15-24).

In that he represents man, this passage reads like an analysis of the demoniac's state. In so far as we tend towards evil, and this tendency is frequently indulged, we are "outside ourselves". We can understand what this means if we listen to ourselves talking to ourselves. Surely we have all had the experience of being so divided against ourselves that we start a dialogue. How could you? What on earth were you thinking about? Who are you actually? In this way we distance ourselves from ourselves to a certain extent. We question ourselves by questioning our own identity. The story of the demoniac illustrates that we can only find our identity by turning towards another person. Paul has the same insight in his postscript to his letter: "Wretched man that I am! Who will deliver me from this body of death?" Yes, who? The answer: "Thanks be to God through Jesus Christ our Lord!" (Rom 7,24f).

After all that we have said perhaps it is now clear that having to imagine the devil and demons as *personified powers* is not important, and in some ways it is inappropriate. Of course the demonic is personal, to the extent that it always attaches itself to a human being. But we sense that evil dwells within us, and that we are drawn to it. We do not need sly "insinuations" from beyond or weird arts of temptation performed by "personified" demons whom we can blame for our misdemeanors. And we also know we need redeeming and are capable of being redeemed. If we are professed Christians we hold fast to the fact that evil cannot endure before Christ, and that he has opened a way for each one of us that will lead us to God, and at *the same time* to ourselves, to awareness of our own identity. This awareness is fundamental to Christian belief. When we acknowledge it we have grasped what the Holy Scriptures are *actually* about when they speak of the devil or demons.

Dostoevski expresses this in "The Possessed." Stepan Trofimovitch Verhovensky, another intellectual, represents a positive alternative to Nikolay Stavrogin. When he recognizes the destructive violence that he stood for in his youth, he goes through an inner transformation. He makes a pilgrimage through the country and comes into contact with the deeply-rooted faith of the simple people. On his deathbed he asks someone to read him the story of the healing of the demoniac of Gerasa. Only then does he understand the sense of this extraordinary passage that had been a stumbling block to him all his life.

That is exactly like our Russia - these devils that are driven out of the sick man into the swine. They are all the plagues, the miasmas, all the impurities...that have amassed in our beloved invalid, our Russia, in the course of ages and ages...The sick man will be healed, and sit at the feet of Jesus.

Dostoevski expresses his conviction that faith in God alone is able to protect man from self-destruction. And indeed, if we sit at Jesus's feet and look up to him we need not give the nature of the demonic another thought. Our hearts will be filled by him whose presence always robs the demon of his power.

5
"It is not I who act"

The Healing of the Young Man with a Dumb Spirit (Mk 9,14-29)

Overcome by emotion or aggression we insult or humiliate or shout at someone we actually like or at least want to treat with respect. In retrospect we almost die of shame. We are astonished that we could forget ourselves to such an extent. We are tempted to say: "That was not I." Who was it then?

The Search for Merit

Francois Mauriac, French novelist and Nobel Prize winner, was familiar with the labyrinthine ways of the human psyche and the darkness of the human soul. In his novel "The Woman of the Pharisees" he draws a picture of a woman called Brigitte Pian, a lady dedicated to charitable acts, who incessantly weaves her web of merits. When she considers the weaknesses of her fellow human beings it is not hard for her to thank God for her own virtues, although it is difficult to say whether she does this through her arrogance or her sense of self-justification.

Among others, Brigitte Pian looks after the Puybarauds, a poverty-stricken young couple. She pays the rent for their flat. They fear her visits which are more like inspections, especially one day when her eye lights on a piano.

"It is odd," she said, "But somehow I don't remember that piano in the inventory which was sent me when I took these

rooms for you."

"No," replied Octavia in a voice that trembled, "it is a piece of silliness for which I am alone responsible."

She looked at the elder woman with that sweet, disarming smile which few could resist. But the expression of hauteur on the face of her patroness showed no sign of softening.

"Forgive me darling," broke in Monsieur Puybaraud, "it was I who suggested it, and I was thinking more about my own pleasure than yours."

It was foolish of him to call his wife 'darling' in front of Brigitte Pian. She had always hated the lack of reserve in married couples who, presuming on the legitimacy of such endearments, stressed by word and gesture the fact of their squalid intimacy. In the case of this particular pair it was quite intolerable.

"Am I to understand," she enquired in tones that were suspiciously gentle, "that you have hired this piano?"

The accused nodded.

"One of you, then, must be capable of giving music lessons. I had an idea that you were both so ignorant of the art as not even to know your notes."

Octavia explained that they had agreed to give themselves this small indulgence. [1]

In a somewhat contemptuous way Brigitte Pian lets the Puybarauds know that they cannot afford any indulgences if they live off other people's alms.

At this Monsieur Puybaraud allowed himself to be carried away by one of those sudden outbursts of temper to which weak natures are prone. Seeing that Brigitte was already on the landing, he exclaimed rather too loudly:

"After all, darling, this is our house isn't it?"...

Such an easy triumph enabled her to recover an almost divine complacency. The statement with which she had just silenced her wretched adversary stood in no need of being elaborated. But she could not resist the temptation of leveling a parting shot.

"Would you like me to send you the lease? You will find, I think, that the name in which it is drawn up is not yours!"

Brigitte Pian was no sooner in the street than she turned what remained of her anger against herself. How could she so utterly have lost control of her temper? What would the Puybarauds think? They did not, as she did, see her perfections from within, nor could they measure the height, breadth and depth of her virtue. They would judge her in the light of an outburst which, if the truth were told, had made her feel thoroughly ashamed. How could human nature be relied upon, she thought... if after a whole lifetime spent in the conquest of herself, at an age when she might reasonably expect to be exempt from the weaknesses which disgusted her in others, the mere sight of a piano was enough to break down all her self-control?

Though the maintenance of her armor of perfection was one of her most constant preoccupations, there was nothing so very extraordinary in a link occasionally working loose. She could always console herself for such an occurrence - provided no witness had been by. But the Puybarauds, especially Octavia, were the last people in the world before whom she would willingly have shown signs of weakness.

Whenever we act against our convictions we are tempted to interpret our bad behavior as an embarrassing weakness, an unnecessary faux pas or a mistake that could have been avoided. Like Brigitte Pian, we probably do not regret losing our patience as much as losing our prestige. It is not so much the hurt we have inflicted on another person but our own hurt pride that bothers us, along with the fact that we have not managed to clamber up another rung of the ladder of perfection *by our own boot straps*. We feel bad not because we are bad, but because we have given in to a bad tendency.

However the Bible sees this the other way round. It stands the principle of cause and effect on its head. Man is not bad because he does evil, but rather, because he gives in to his wicked tendencies over and over again, he is fundamentally a wrongdoer. By reason of this constitutional flaw he is quite unable to bring about anything good of himself.

Mark tells us a miracle story in his gospel that expresses this very clearly.

And when they came to the disciples (Jesus, Peter, James and John), they saw a great crowd about them, and scribes arguing with them. And immediately all the crowd, when they saw him, were greatly amazed, and ran up to him and greeted him. And he asked them, "What are you discussing with them?" And one of the crowd answered him, "Teacher, I brought my son to you, for he has a dumb spirit; and wherever it seizes him, it dashes him down; and he foams at the mouth and grinds his teeth and becomes rigid; and I asked your disciples to cast it out, and they were not able." And he answered them "O faithless generation, how long am I to bear with you? Bring him to me." And they brought the boy to him; and when the spirit saw him, immediately it convulsed the boy, and he fell on the ground and rolled about, foaming at the mouth. And Jesus asked his father, "How long has he had this?" And he said "From childhood. It has often cast him into the fire and into the water, to destroy him, but if you can do anything, have pity on us if you can and help us." And Jesus said to him "If you can? All things are possible to him who believes." Immediately the father of the child cried out and said "I believe, help my unbelief!" And when

Jesus saw the crowd come running together, he rebuked the unclean spirit, saying to it, "You dumb and deaf spirit, I command you, come out of him, and never enter him again." And after crying out and convulsing him terribly, it came out, and the boy was like a corpse; so that most of them said, "He is dead." But Jesus took him by the hand and lifted him up, and he arose. And when he had entered the house, his disciples asked him privately, "Why could we not cast it out?" And he said to them, "This kind cannot be driven out by anything but prayer." (Mk 9,14-29).

One or two basic points can help us to understand this account. First of all we have to remember that when demons and exorcism are linked together in the gospels, people are not talking about the devil, but about evil spirits. Jesus's exorcisms are not aimed at the devil, at God's actual adversary, but at those "negative spirits" (or as Fridolin Stier calls them, "Abergeister"[2]) who according to a then prevailing belief played evil games with mankind. We must also remember that the biblical authors were bound to give *their* world view which was not overly skeptical. And their world view was far removed from ours. In fact in those days, illnesses that were inexplicable - and this was true not only of the biblical world - were traced back to the influence of demons. A paucity of medical knowledge led people to make do with theological "diagnoses". And those nearest to hand pointed to possession.

Possession or Illness?

These theological interpretations were part of the order of the day, but they seem quite foreign to us now. However we should not overlook the fact that they are even today widespread in some circles, when the emphasis is shifted from

142

the medical to the psychical. Such believers refuse to relate personality disturbances to physical illness, and instead expect a "supernatural" explanation. Quite often it is the person afflicted who, unconsciously, tends to interpret a psychic disturbance or illness as demonic. I have a case to illustrate this.[3]

A psychiatrist who is at a loss about a young woman patient asks a priest to see her. The patient who has an eating disorder has refused all medical help, but is prepared to go to confession to a priest and reveal her trouble. The priest learns from her that she has signed a pact with the devil. If he can help her to become so fat through over-eating that she will eventually burst, she will grant him her soul.

Research into this case establishes that the woman is suffering from extreme weariness of life because she has always had a raw deal and been treated badly. She is almost literally eaten up by rage. Unconsciously she wants to bring this to the attention of her fellow human beings by parading it before their eyes. They must see that they are responsible for her misery. They do not like her, they can't stand her, they have ruined her.

The pact with the devil is nothing more than the result of other people condemning this young woman: they say she is quite crazy, or mad, and she should go to the devil! And this confirms the pact. The woman feels rejected, and this rejection (real or imagined) drives her into isolation. For their part her fellow human beings spurn her; after all, who feels at ease in the company of a "strange person?"

Doctors and priests constantly have similar experiences. People who have been repressed and have not learnt to defend themselves imagine that others are evil, or they absorb other people's ideas and think of themselves as evil. This means that the more we exclude a suffering, repressed,

143

*and sick person from the community, the more we allow him
or her to become the opposite of the "normal" human being,
the scapegoat, the villain, who we think is responsible
himself for all his woes. All that is left to him is the role of
the outsider into which we have violently pushed him.*

*The devil in this story does not enter by chance, he is also
the echo, the being who resonates the exclusive behavior of
the others. The pact with the devil signals the final resistance,
even though it is made in a state of despair and powerlessness. In our case the priest was able to accept the ambivalent
feelings of the young woman. She trusted him, and he helped
to bring her back into the community, patiently, step by step.
To this extent the devil left her and the pact was broken.*

*It is easy to understand. In reality it was not this woman but
her fellow human beings who isolated her, who (seen biblically) gave the devil room in her heart. To exclude a person
from the community, to give him up, brand him, "drive him
to the devil" is in reality a sign that we cannot handle him
or his way of thinking, his suffering. We are afraid of
becoming infected by him, being drawn in, becoming unclean
or sick ourselves.*[4]

Just as we can get nearer to this young woman, we can also
try to give a name to the young man's "possession" in
Mark's story. All his symptoms point to epilepsy; he is
overcome by convulsions, a force that throws him to the
ground, and he foams at the mouth. He grinds his teeth and
then becomes rigid. After his collapse he is totally exhausted,
just like a corpse.

In 430 B.C. Hippocrates, the founder of Greek medicine,
wrote a paper about "the sacred disease", in which he tried
to explain from a scientific point of view the sickness we
know today as epilepsy. His theory had little impact then.
Later it also failed to command attention, largely due to the

spiritual writer Origen (c. 185-253/4), who wrote about the healing of the epileptic boy in his commentary to Matthew's gospel: "Doctors want to find a natural explanation, and are convinced that no unclean spirit is involved, but that we are dealing with an appearance of sickness in the body... However we believe with the gospel that the boy afflicted was obviously (!) affected by an unclean, dumb and deaf spirit."[5]

Today if we substitute the gospel's tacitly assumed demonic interpretation (which Origen supports) with a medical finding, we can establish that Jesus was not casting out a negative spirit but healing a sick man. Furthermore there is the question whether this story merely served as a narrative illustration of Jesus's person and his message, or whether an actual historical event lies behind it. There is some evidence of the latter.[6] The story does not follow any previous pattern (which is usually the case in accounts of miracles), but has individual features. I refer particularly to the detailed description of the boy's illness. The christological formulae found in other miracle stories are also lacking. These are generally theological interpretations of the figure of Jesus written by the early Christian community or the evangelists; see Mk 1,24, where the evangelist puts a confession of faith into the mouth of the negative spirit: "I know who you are, the Holy One of God."

These points may not be entirely unimportant for research into Jesus's life. But they are certainly not in the foreground when we start to reflect on the significance of the story of the epileptic boy in *our* belief. Then the decisive question is whether and how we ourselves come out in the episode.

At the Mercy of Evil

In fact the whole story is actually about us! But rest assured, the evangelist does not want to lecture us about whether we should imagine demons as personified beings or abstract forces. That is our problem! During his lifetime there was no argument about it. He is more concerned about a thoroughly unacademic subject; we are all at the mercy of evil in one way or another. And Jesus can save us from it. As we hear from the disciples' last question ("Why could we not cast it out?") they had tried in vain to heal the boy before Jesus arrived. This shows that all help must come from Jesus.

We recognize ourselves in this story as soon as we realize that the boy with convulsions represents humankind. Man is neither free to reject evil nor to overcome it. From the first moment of his existence he is at its mercy. He has no power over evil *in himself* because it took hold of him a long time ago.

This is the Bible's interpretation from the first sentences steeped in myth right through to Paul's thoughtful and sensitive letters. Paul refers to his personal experiences when he complains that he does not understand his own actions: "For I do not do what I want, but I do the very thing I hate" (Rom 7,15).

It is worth noting that Paul does not refer to his change in life *before* Damascus. He is speaking about his human frailty in general. He had always been zealous, even before he converted to Christianity, and he remained so until the end of his life. His experience is the same as ours; his will and his behavior, his endeavors and his actions are constantly at war with each other: "So then it is no longer I that do it, but sin which dwells within me" (Rom 7,15). This means that I am no longer master of myself in my own house, sin has the last word, *it* guides me, *it* activates me, *it* wins through.

Paul is not thinking at all about relativizing or smoothing out man's responsibility, nor is he negating it. It is I myself who have ripped open the gap between the "I" that wants the good, and the "I" that does evil. It is not a question of

146

the degree of responsibility, but the experience of a radical decline into evil.

Purely logical categories prove insufficient in analyzing this sort of experience. We can express our horror, but it is impossible to be articulate about them.

Many thinkers and poets have gone through these experiences, and reflected on the nature of man and his identity. I remember the Italian writer Elio Vittorini and his novel "Men and Not Men." He describes a shocking scene when a captain lets his dogs tear a soldier to pieces because the soldier has shot one of the dogs in self-defence. Vittorini ends this terrible description with the following thoughts:

"Man," one says. And we think of someone fallen, or lost, of someone who cries and who is hungry, of him who is cold, sick, persecuted, of him who is put to death. We think of the wrong he is made to endure, and of his dignity. And of all in him that is offended, of the capacity he has for happiness. That is man.

We presume that mankind includes only what men experience and what we expect as part of man's lot. To be hungry—that, we say, is human. To be cold. And to be rid of hunger, to leave cold behind, to inhale the air of the earth and to have hold of it in one's lungs, to have the earth, trees, rivers, grain, cities, to vanquish the wolf and look the world in the eye. That, we say, belongs to what is human....

But man can also get along without anything inside him, neither want nor expectation, neither hunger nor cold; but that, we say, is not human.

We consider him. He is like unto a wolf. He attacks and ravages. And we say: This is no man. He acts in cold blood as does the wolf. But does this remove him from among mankind? we think only of the offended.

No sooner is there offense than we side with the offended,

and we say the offended are mankind. Do they bleed? Behold
mankind. Do tears flow? Behold mankind.
  And he who offends—what is he?
  We never think that he too is man. Whatever else could he
be? Wolf?[7]

Auschwitz and the Pastoral Symphony were both created
by men. Man is indeed capable of almost everything. He is
not only able to reach unimaginable heights, but is hurled
(or hurls himself) into the deepest, darkest abyss. The
psalmist describes this conflict. What is man? A thing of
nothing! "But I am a worm, and no man" (Ps 22,6). And
then again, thinking of his destiny and looking towards God
he says, "What is man that thou art mindful of him?...Yet
thou hast made him little less than God, and dost crown him
with glory and honor. Thou hast given him dominion over
the works of thy hands; thou hast put all things under his
feet..." (Ps 8,4-6).
  And yet it is impossible to divide man into two groups, into
good and evil. The break is within each individual; one and
the same person unites both within himself, splendor and
misery, magnificence and wretchedness, the yearning for
purity and the tendency towards crime. The Russian novelist
Tolstoy (1828-1910) writes about this in his book "Resurrection":

It is one of the most usual and widespread superstitions that
every person has only one specific characteristic of his own,
that a person is either good or bad or clever or stupid or
energetic or apathetic and so on. But people are not like that.
Although we can say of a person that he is more often good
than evil, more often clever than stupid, more often energetic
than apathetic or the other way round, it is inaccurate to say
that one person is good or clever, and that another is evil or

148

stupid. And yet we always divide people up like this. It is wrong. People are like rivers; the water is the same everywhere, it is the same water, but every river is suddenly narrow and rushing, suddenly broad and still, suddenly clean and cold, suddenly muddied and warm. It is the same with people. Every person carries within himself the seed of all human characteristics, sometimes he shows one, sometimes another, and often he even seems to himself to be unlike himself, and yet, he is always the same person.[8]

The French natural scientist and mathematician Blaise Pascal (1623-1662) expresses himself more pointedly: "This man that has been born to know the universe, to judge all things, to administer a whole state, is now busy and quite absorbed in hunting a hare."[9] Goethe's Faust speaks of this in images; there are "two souls" that dwell within his breast.[10] Hermann Hesse illustrates the same theme in his novel "Narziss und Goldmund". Both these characters symbolize one person and are torn between sensuality and spirituality.

Basic human experiences are reflected in all these statements. We all recognize ourselves in them in one way or another. And these texts also make it easier for us to understand Mark's story, which underlines man's decline into evil in that the demon and the boy seem to merge into one person. Man is helpless faced with this evil, he is bewildered, and above all speechless. It is not by chance that the negative spirit overpowering the boy is dumb. How significant it is that the boy's father only functions as a mouthpiece and interpreter for his dumb child, who has literally been left speechless by this evil. *Seen theologically*, the father is a kind of Doppelgänger—the ghostly double of a living person—and he expresses this when he says to Jesus "Have pity on us!"

149

The boy represents all those unbelievers described by Jesus who are at the mercy of evil. What happens to the boy also happens to them; the demon hurls them constantly to the ground, into the filth. But the boy has always lain there. "From childhood" is the father's reply to Jesus's question "How long has he had this?". This is not a biographical detail but a theological statement. In fact man is at the mercy of hostile powers right from the beginning, so that he sees death in everything - even the fire that warms us and the water that gives us life become threats. According to the father the demon "has often cast him into the fire and into the water to destroy him."

This fall of man into evil is one of the main themes in the Holy Scriptures, where evil, according to the Bible, has its origins in human misbehavior. Of course it is futile to speculate on what man's first sin could have been. We know that the story of the Fall is not an historical report but an ethological reconstruction. The biblical writer was looking for the cause (Greek: aitía = cause, reason) of an experience that he and his contemporaries knew only too well - man tends towards evil and inflicts it upon others, so bringing about new suffering. Because man eats from the tree of knowledge (Gen 2,17; of course this story is written in the language of imagery) he puts himself in God's place; he determines what is good and evil for himself, so evoking pain and death (Gen 3,14-19).

Through his sin he rebels against God's instructions entrusted to him for his own good. Logically enough, this breach leads to a breakdown in human relationship. Immediately after he has sinned, Adam distances himself from Eve, who is bone of his bone, flesh of his flesh (Gen 2,23). "The woman whom thou gavest to be with me, she gave me the fruit of the tree, and I ate" (Gen 3,12). It is the first account of man dissembling about his guilt and it then becomes the story of an excuse, at the expense of another person. So the biblical writer shows us where the actual power of evil lies, how it works on inexorably, how it develops its own dynamic in man's egoism. The foul deed can be compared to a stone thrown into a lake. At first the ripples form small circles that gradually widen until they cover a great expanse of water. In this way the breach in human relationships is extended beyond Adam to his sons. Cain murders Abel (Gen 4,8). Man's violent deeds grow even more violent, as we hear in the wild song of Lamech, one of Cain's descendants: "I have slain a man for wounding me, a young man for striking me. If Cain is avenged sevenfold, truly Lamech seventy-sevenfold." (Gen 4,23f)

The catastrophic results brought about by evil are elucidated in the introduction to the story of the Flood: "The Lord saw that the wickedness of man was great in the earth, and that every imagination of the thoughts of his heart was only evil continually" (Gen 6,5).

Because the biblical authors were working within their own experiences and projecting these onto the past, it is not surprising that, as a result of their accounts, the later history of Israel is an exact repetition of man's history from the beginning. Like the first man, the people of Israel are showered with gifts from God. And like Adam, the people revoke their obedience to God. Almost all the prophets, constantly in danger of their lives, draw attention to this. Hosea (c. 750 B.C.) proclaims:

There is no faithfulness or kindness,
and no knowledge of God in the land;
there is swearing, lying, killing,
stealing, and committing adultery;
they break all bounds and murder
follows murder.
(Hos 4,1f; compare Is 59,12-14).

151

It is Love alone that counts

To some extent the timeless, existential significance of the story of the boy who was possessed illustrates these human experiences of evil. The disciples' question "Why could we not cast it out?" means that in despair the father had turned first to them, but in vain. His hope was based upon human power. But the evangelist emphasizes that this is not enough, and rescue comes solely from Jesus. He alone is superior to all the forces of death. This is behind Jesus's reply to the disciples: "This kind (of negative spirit) cannot be driven out by anything but prayer." But prayer is nothing less than faith put into words. Obviously this is where the "faithless generation" breaks down. Jesus is not primarily concerned about his countrymen's individual sins against God; what he accuses them of is their lack of trust in God. And the evangelist accuses his readers of the same thing. The individual misdemeanors that make us guilty are simply a *result* of this lack, a concrete expression of the unbelief that Jesus deplores.

It is only when we turn towards Jesus, and therefore towards God, that we experience the real meaning of life; for "There is salvation in no one else" (Acts 4,12). This statement from the Acts of the Apostles is developed in the narration of the story of the boy possessed.

It is only faith (and by this the evangelist means the active and usually banal day by day following of Jesus) that can overcome evil. The demon leaving the boy at Jesus's command signifies that man, with his limited means and strength, is never able to defeat evil alone. The only force that can prevail against the power of evil is the power of grace, and this is always effective when a believer allows himself to be led by God. Such faith is open to doubts and at the mercy of uncertainty. We hear this in the father's confession—again

152

as a mouthpiece for his son: "I believe; help my unbelief!"

Help my unbelief. This means that the father sees belief as a gift that cannot be understood as a result of human effort. The man fallen into evil can do nothing good of himself; whatever he does is under the sign of death.

This is what Francois Mauriac's Woman of the Pharisees overlooks. She will not accept salvation, but thinks it must be purchased, as if God were for sale, and we could earn heaven. But her self-justifying attitude does not remain entirely immune to the challenge of grace. After she has left the Puybarauds to go to confession in the cathedral, and to recover her presumed peace of mind, she has a vague intimation that her present striving for piety will never lead to God:

There were days... when a flash of lightning would tear holes in the mists that shrouded her soul, and show her to herself as she really was. When that happened, she realized, beyond all possibility of denial (the mood never lasted for more than a moment) that her way of life was not the only way of life, nor her God the only God. The sense of satisfaction in being Brigitte Pian, which as a rule, was so overpowering, fell away from her suddenly, and she shivered, feeling herself naked and miserable, cast upon an arid waste of sand beneath a copper sky. Far away she could hear angelic choirs, and mingled with them the hateful voices of the Puybarauds.

But she suppresses this knowledge immediately.

The feeling soon passed, and she always managed, by dint of certain impromptu prayers of proved efficacy, to recover her spiritual equilibrium. When the need for such rehabilitation came on her, she would pause before an altar some-

153

where (as now in the cathedral) until silence once more filled her heart. She not only felt the silence, but adored it as a sign sent to her from her hidden Master that she had again found grace in His eyes. But today, first before the Holy Sacrament and later before the statue of the Virgin which stands behind the choir (looking for all the world like the Empress Eugénie), she was conscious of a voice within her that spoke in tones of disapproval. "It has been sent to try me" she thought; "I must submit in all humility" which was her way of saying "Notice, I beg, O Lord, that I do not kick against the pricks, and enter my acquiescence, please, on the credit side of the account."

It is only much later that Brigitte Pian struggles towards the conviction that holiness does not come from arduous works of faith, but is an undeserved grace, a pure gift, and that in the end there is nothing left except to leave everything, really everything, to "the Great Compassion."

In the evening of her life, Brigitte Pian had come to the knowledge that it is useless to play the part of a proud servitor eager to impress his master by a show of readiness to repay his debts to the last farthing. It had been revealed to her that our Father does not ask us to give a scrupulous account of what merits we can claim. She understood at last that it is not our just desserts that matter but our love.

Mauriac's novel is an exact paraphrase of the story of the possessed boy, in that Brigitte Pian finally realizes that if man acts of his own accord, things will go badly. But if he places his trust in God, all manner of things will be well in the end. In other words, Brigitte takes the step from death into life.

How does man achieve this step? It is actually the question

that lies within the story of the possessed boy, and the story gives us an answer.

The boy seemed to be dead, "But Jesus took him by the hand and lifted him up, and he arose." In fact Mark is describing an awakening from the dead, and saying that the Lord of life and death can conquer all the forces of darkness and give us life. But it can also be said that a society in which nothing is given to us is deathly. However we can all allow ourselves to receive gifts in the meeting with Jesus, who creates life.

6
Pour out good Wine!

The Marriage of Cana (Jn 2,1-12)

Reading some of the events in the New Testament can make us a little envious of Jesus's contemporaries because we were not there. As a child I thought about this when the story of the marriage of Cana was read to me for the first time. The place was not important - if someone had told me that Cana was probably Khirbet Kana which lies a good 13 kilometers north of Nazareth - I would probably have forgotten this immediately. A few miserable ruins of the town have survived. What interested me was the incredible event.

In the meantime I have naturally learnt that we have to read texts extremely carefully to avoid wrong interpretations.

On the third day there was a marriage at Cana in Galilee, and the mother of Jesus was there; Jesus was also invited to the marriage, with his disciples. When the wine gave out, the mother of Jesus said to him, "They have no wine." And Jesus said to her, "Woman, what has this concern of yours to do with me? My hour has not yet come." His mother said to the servants, "Do whatever he tells you." Now six stone jars were standing there, for the Jewish rites of purification, each holding twenty or thirty gallons. Jesus said to them, "Fill the jars with water." And they filled them up to the brim. He said to them, "Now draw some out, and take it to the steward of the feast." So they took it. When the steward of the feast tasted the water now become wine, and did not know where it came from, (though the servants that had drawn the water knew), the steward of the feast called the bridegroom and said to him, "Every man serves the good wine first; and when men have drunk freely, then the poor wine; but you have kept the good wine until now." This, the first of his signs, Jesus did at Cana in Galilee, and manifested his glory; and his disciples believed in him (Jn 2,1-11).

Inconsistencies

Even readers with an unquestioning belief in miracles need some time to reflect upon this one. The narrator has left us with an astonishing event that must have amazed his listeners too, and there are some puzzling details.

For example, the main actors do not appear. The steward calls the bridegroom to account, but we never hear a word about the bride. Their part in the story is insignificant.

The way Jesus addresses his mother is also rather strange: "Woman!" And then he goes on to say: "What has this to do with me?" Bible interpreters have been trying to work this out for centuries. In the meantime we know that this method of address was common at the time. We can translate it as; "Leave me in peace!" or "What do you want?" (in the way that the Italians say *"Ma cosa vuoi?"*) Jesus is simply letting his mother know that she has no influence over his messianic mission. It is interesting that John never mentions her name in his gospel. Jesus calling her "woman" was neither diminishing her nor insulting her. John puts the same word into Jesus's mouth at the hour of his death, when he trusts his mother to the care of the disciple whom he loved: "Woman, behold your son!" (Jn 19,26).

Contrary to a widespread assumption, the text does not imply that Mary asks Jesus for a miracle. She simply makes

157

him aware of a situation that could be embarrassing for the bridal pair, and rather annoying for the guests. However *she does not exclude* the fact that her son can help, as is clear in her remarks to the servants.

But Jesus hears something quite different in her comment. From his point of view, his mother expects him to reveal himself now as the savior. But he cannot fulfill this expectation. "My hour has not yet come." From the evangelist's theological point of view, *this* hour is the hour of the Passion, and only the Father can determine when and how it will come to pass. This is quite unmistakable in the prayer that John puts into Jesus's mouth before he is arrested: "Father, *the hour* has come; glorify thy Son that the Son may glorify thee..." (Jn 17,1).

These complications may come from the fact that John referred back to a manuscript that was not available to the other evangelists. It was largely an account of miracles. The experts call this the Semeion source (from the Greek word *semeion* meaning miracle or sign). Apart from the miracle of Cana, it has accounts of at least six other miracles.[1]

The fourth evangelist—many scholars claim that he was not identical with the apostle John, and only wrote his manuscript at about the end of the first century—probably took over this source, edited it and incorporated it into his work. Like the other evangelists, he adopted a theological point of view. This means that he did not simply copy the miracle stories from his source, but commented on them.

An example of this is his explanation of the six stone jars. John was obviously writing for an audience that was not familiar with Jewish instructions, and so felt obliged to refer to them: "Now six stone jars were standing there, for the Jewish rites of purification..."

These stone water jars were used for physical hygiene and ritual cleansing. For example, one had to wash one's hands before and after meals, and after returning from the market place or another district where one could come into unclean contact with non-Jews. There were also strict regulations about cleaning crockery and vessels.

If we want to understand how the story continues, we need to visualize what the narrator *does not* say. The bridal pair were poor, the guests had drunk a great deal, and Jesus and his relations and his disciples only turned up at the last moment. Perhaps they were not *all* invited, putting the hosts into a quandary. Jesus would then have come to their aid out of simple decency.

We are also justified in assuming that this was a simple village wedding. These often extended over many days, far longer than even a prince could afford today. A wedding with a virgin went on for seven days, while a widow who re-married had to be content with three days.[2] Not all the guests were there all the time. Gifts from those invited were presented at the marriage feast, just as chocolate rabbits are given to children in Germany at Easter, and Christmas cakes in Britain are bought from Marks and Spencer to celebrate the feast.

It would be unkind to assume that people drank too much at the village feast in Cana. Of course the wine flowed. And the evangelist found it self-evident that some guests went too far (..."when men have drunk freely"). There is a passage from the Talmud that refers to this. Even the rabbis emptied their goblets happily, drinking toasts to themselves and their disciples, and sometimes their inebriated state had a disastrous effect on the precious and fragile drinking vessels. The custom of breaking glasses at a wedding seems to go back to this time.

It is not really worth speculating about the lack of wine. The evangelist says simply that something essential to the joy of a wedding was lacking.

Jesus did not only confine himself to dealing with *the essential.* There were six huge stone jars full of water, each containing about 80 to 120 liters, and he turns these into wine. At a rough estimate that would produce between 480 and 720 liters. We are also talking about a very special wine, if we can believe the steward. This can be taken with a certain amount of humor, because this rule of serving wine, "(Every man serves the good wine first")" is not referred to anywhere else in the ancient world.

However there are certain analogies between this miracle story and the widespread legend of Dionysus in the ancient world. Dionysus (Bacchus in Latin) was the God of wine. His feast was celebrated on January 6, and in some of the temples dedicated to him, wine was handed round. It was said that the God had changed water into this wine. We should also mention a popular custom in Elis, a district to the north west of the Peloponnesus. During the evening before the feast of Dionysus three empty stone jars were put into the God's sanctuary. Then the doors were locked. In the morning the stone jars were filled with wine.[3] Some Bible scholars think it is possible that this custom had some influence on the story of the miracle of Cana. But that does not exclude the fact that *the evangelist himself* found his source in the Semeion, and most probably did not only understand it as imagery, but as literal truth.

A Chinese Parable

However the real problem is not whether John interpreted the miracle of Cana symbolically or literally; *what he actually wanted to say in the story is crucial.*

It strikes us that no one was surprised by this spectacular event, although the vast amount of wine would have been enough to put a whole company of hardened drinkers under the table. It is also a characteristic of New Testament gift miracles not to arouse any astonishment in those present, because the wondrous effect of the miracle is simply hinted at (in contrast to miracles of healing).[4] Although the evangelist is describing an extraordinary occurrence, he is not concerned about the spectacle. A historical enquiry would be justified in trying to reconstruct Jesus's character, but it would not benefit what the author is trying to say. We do not have to fathom *the meaning of the miracle in itself, but the intention behind it.*

To do this we have to return to a problem briefly mentioned before.[5] Jesus's mother points out that they have no more wine. Jesus understands her remark to mean that he should accomplish his work of redemption now. However the "hour" in which this will happen depends alone upon the will of the Father. Meanwhile it is left to Jesus's will to do something else. And so he performs a sign through which he will reveal both his majesty and the meaning of his whole future work in advance, giving his followers to understand what he expects of them; namely *that they too will change water into wine.*

This would seem to be the real and only reason why John tells us this story.

Before we go any deeper into this thought - and not only comment on the gospel but bring it up to date - I would like to look at another story that comes from an entirely different time and culture. It is a Chinese parable.

A bridal pair got ready to celebrate their wedding. Although they were poor they wanted many people to share their happiness. But how could they, poor as they were, celebrate without good wine, the symbol of joyous feasting? They discussed this for a long time, and finally came to what they thought was a clever decision. They invited all their friends and neighbors to the marriage feast, and asked them to bring their own wine as a wedding gift.

The wedding day dawned, the bride and groom were full of joy as they awaited their guests. The long tables were simple, but decorated for the occasion, and music played. The guests appeared, and one after another they poured the wine they had brought into huge stone jars that stood at the entrance, so that they were filled to the brim.

The feast began and the bridegroom waved to those who had offered to serve the guests. They should now carry up the precious drink. So they went with their jugs to fill them from the stone jars, and then poured the wine out carefully for the bride and groom and all those invited. The guests raised their cups ceremoniously to drink the bridal pair's health. They were full of expectation as they tasted the sweet wine.

But then suddenly the bride began to weep, and the bridegroom gazed in horror at the company. The hall was deathly still. The guests bowed their heads, and stared at the ground. No one had believed this, but they all now saw it clearly before them; no wine sparkled in the cups but pure water.

Obviously every visitor had thought that if they poured a little water into the massive jars no one would notice. The water that they had brought would mix easily with the wine of the others.

The bridegroom put his arm round his bride, and while he tried to comfort her with soft words, the guests stood up and left the hall in great shame without the feast taking place at all.[6]

The story of the marriage of Cana and the parable of the "water miracle" are like chalk and cheese. But they can both be applied to the Church, to my mind with some success.

In the opinion of the evangelist, changing water into wine is the task that was given to the Church. He reminds his readers of this in the story of the wine miracle of Cana. The Church has never done justice to this task and never will. She has mostly administered the wine of the gospel in a watered-down form to a humanity looking for meaning and orientation, because she does not represent an abstract greatness, but is made up of sinful human beings whose moral blinkers and spiritual narrowness are so obvious that only the dazzled - that is the blind - cannot see this.

The Church - a miserable Organization?

It is not my intention here to offset the great chronicle of services done by officially recognized saints against Karlheinz Deschner's "Criminal History of Christianity" and the list of misdeeds committed by church officials. It would be impossible and anyway quite meaningless.

The Church has brought forth so much good in the hearts of men during the course of centuries. And this same Church has both allowed and caused so much pain, not only in society but also in the souls of individual people. This Church that not only proclaims the salvation announced by Jesus but also embodies it, if only approximately, has always allowed herself to be dazzled by her own sense of mission. It has sometimes led to her being fanatical and blind to the signs of the times, so that she has often caused disaster where she could have alleviated or averted it by helping and healing. Right from the start, the Church's preaching and practice have contained discrepancies between ideal and reality, and this is the reason why she has been judged in such varied ways.

What is the Church? An old catechism answered this question succinctly: "The Church is the Kingdom of God on

Earth."[7]

"The Church? What is it?" Friedrich Nietzsche put this question in his "Thus Spake Zarathustra". Nietzsche's answer was: "The Church is a kind of state, and in fact it is the most mendacious."[8]

We have good reason to contradict Nietzsche's observation, but this does not mean that we therefore have to agree with the catechism answer. We can be completely loyal to the Church, and at the same time distance ourselves from this "chauvinistic Catholicism." There is a response to such self-congratulation in a sermon preached by a theologian: "If I am asked what I think of the Catholic Church then I am only too happy to say: 'I think of the Catholic Church as a miserable organization; but I don't know of a better one because I believe that in spite of everything, God comes to meet me in her. I love this Church, and in spite of all her problems, as far as I can be with my feeble strength, I am totally committed to her."

Adolf Exeler[9] who died some years ago, preached this sermon, and some of his congregation took it very badly. They found it out of place and unjust to speak of the Church in this disrespectful way.

Disrespectful? Unjust? We say the "Our Father" regularly, at least in church on Sundays. We pray for the *coming* of his kingdom, for the strength to *be able to* fulfill his will, and we also pray for *the forgiveness* of our sins.

We are not just praying for ourselves, but for all the community of the faithful and therefore the Church. She is not only made up of the Pope and the bishops and the priests and their curates - if they have them anymore. The Church is all of us that are baptized and believe in Jesus Christ. When we are aware of this, have we considered how critical the "Our Father" is of the Church?

Thy kingdom come! It is precisely this request that the

Church has not understood nearly enough in her self-criticism. As long as we pray for the coming of the kingdom of God, we are admitting that God's kingdom has not come. Instead of seeing this, the Church has sometimes been alarmingly assured of herself in her identification with God's kingdom. If the Church were "the kingdom of God on earth" as the catechism we have mentioned says (almost heretically), then we would not have to say the "Our Father" anymore, every plea for forgiveness would be unnecessary, and every celebration of the Eucharist superfluous. We would not have to celebrate Holy Communion, the anointing of the sick would just be a meaningless ritual, the sacrament of confession a farce. We would not need any more Church marriages, the liturgy and even the smallest impromptu prayer to God would be nothing less than empty affectation. For every sacrament and every moment of prayer, even the lighting of candles before the statues of St Anthony and the Mother of God, do not only serve to profess our faith and bring us nearer to God, but are at the same time obvious signs that God's kingdom is still to come.

They show that the Church cannot possibly be identified with the kingdom of God on earth; her *task* is to strive for it, to realize this kingdom of God *symbolically*, and to draw man's gaze towards it so that his heart remains open, and his way forward is smoothed. For this reason the Church must protect herself from being part of the establishment of this world, or from idealizing her lost position of power out of a sense of nostalgia. The Church is a *stop-gap*. Her work is not the goal (the kingdom of God) but the *way* on which she can move forward towards it. The simple question is then whether she strives to get closer to it, or whether she takes her ease and betrays the gospel, thus distancing herself from the goal. This is a perfectly realistic assessment of her situation, and does not try to hide her glorious history in any way. As long as the Church is aware that she is *on the way*, there is no need for her to repress the thought that God's promise to lead her finally to the goal does not exclude her, at least at times, from taking the wrong turning or going astray.

With this in mind the Fathers of the Church spoke of the *Ecclesia semper reformanda*, that is the Church *constantly in need of reform*. The Second Vatican Council expressed itself in a similar way when it drew attention to God's people of Israel passing through the desert, and spoke of the Church passing through the present world in *search* of the "coming and eternal city" (Heb 13,14).[10]

The Church will reach her goal only when she becomes superfluous, that is, at the end of time. Until then she is on her way. This is why the Council describes her as God's pilgrim people and its affirmation is sober and realistic, and yet full of faith, that "Although the people of God are at the mercy of sin in its members during this earthly pilgrimage, it yet grows in Christ and is gently led by the mysterious will of God until it joyfully reaches the fullness of the glorious majesty in the heavenly Jerusalem."[11]

Until then this Church will have to be content with the fact that we measure her against the standards she proclaims, that is, against the gospels, whenever her credibility is discussed.

This credibility does not only prove itself in the Church practicing what she preaches, but also in her attitude towards human experiences. "The joy and hope, the mourning and fear of people today, especially of all the poor and oppressed are also the joy and hope, the mourning and fear of Christ's disciples, men and women. And there is nothing truly human that does not find an echo in their hearts too."[12] In reality this affirmation from Vatican II is to be understood as a guide line; so should it be!

In order to be able to concentrate on questions—and

perhaps try to answer them—we have to listen to people and be aware of their difficulties and experiences, of their doubts and fears, their hopes and their expectations. Unfortunately some Church officials give us the impression that they know everything already about our worries the world over. There is a danger that they will answer questions no one has asked. As a rule we can recognize this kind of "answer" by its woolly speech, pompous style and unctuous diction.

The Church is *on its way* until the end of time and therefore constantly open to the temptation of fitting in with the Zeitgeist and making the Bible's message more comfortable. Whenever this happens she betrays her task of turning water into wine. And there is always the danger that she will secretly declare herself to be the end when she is merely the means. This implies that she must be entirely and completely at the *service* of people, who all have a right to *pure* wine.

The great Jerome (c 347-419/20) seems to have understood this very well. When someone came to him and expressed his doubts about the story of the Marriage of Cana, the famous Bible interpreter and Doctor of the Church asked him why. "Well, it was such a vast quantity of wine!" replied the man. "Yes," answered Jerome, "and we are still drinking from it."

7

Say Yes to Yourself!

The Healing of the Paralytic (Mk 2,1-12)

There are moments in our lives when it seems as if we are paralysed, especially if we are responsible for or have caused a certain situation.

A young woman meets a nice, well-mannered man, falls in love with him, and a deep relationship develops. Something, she does not know what, prevents her from asking about his circumstances; the right time will come to talk about them, and she does not wish to seem curious. One day she learns by chance that the man is married; of course he should not have kept this from her. When she confronts him with it, he makes it quite clear that he is not contemplating divorce, but that it would be nice if they could go on spending their free time together. The girl is confused when she realizes that he has been *using* her as a plaything merely for the pleasure she could give him. She manages to break away and retain her self-respect.

Another example would be a man who gets involved in a violent quarrel in a pub and in a drunken rage fatally injures his companion. The sheer horror of such a deed comes only later.

How do people react in such situations? Perhaps they stamp their feet on the floor, wring their hands, bang their fists on the door or their heads on the wall. Or they throw the first available thing through the window or break up the apartment. Or they get drunk, and roar out their fury against their

168

indescribable helplessness. Sometimes they end up weeping or laughing uncontrollably.

On first realizing her mistake the woman might even think of going by herself on the holiday they had planned together. And the first reaction of the man who has just killed his friend might be, "who will I play cards with in the future?" But when the first shock has passed and what has really happened dawns with full force, these people are not capable of doing anything. They are capable of *nothing*, unable to collect their thoughts or to put them into any kind of order.

Then gradually despair gives way to dullness and apathy. They creep through the world like shadows, indifferent to everything. Or more accurately, everything becomes indifferent, and a kind of paralysis sets in. What is the way out of such a state?

A Glimpse into the Writer's Workshop.

A story in the New Testament attempts to answer this question.

And when he returned to Capernaum after some days, it was reported that he was at home. And many were gathered together, so that there was no longer room for them, not even about the door; and he was preaching the word to them. And they came, bringing to him a paralytic carried by four men. And when they could not get near him because of the crowd, they removed the roof above him; and when they had made an opening, they let down the pallet on which the paralytic lay. And when Jesus saw their faith, he said to the paralytic, "My son, your sins are forgiven." Now some of the scribes were sitting there, questioning in their hearts, "Why does this man speak thus? It is blasphemy! Who can forgive sins but God alone?" And immediately Jesus, perceiving in his spirit that they thus questioned within themselves, said to them, "Why do you question thus in your hearts? Which is easier, to say to the paralytic, 'Your sins are forgiven,' or to say 'Rise, take up your pallet and walk?' But that you may know that the Son of Man has authority on earth to forgive sins" - he said to the paralytic "I say to you, rise, take up your pallet and go home." And he rose, and immediately took up the pallet and went out before them all, so that they were amazed and glorified God, saying "We never saw anything like this!" (Mk 2,1-12)

It is fairly obvious here that two stories have been slotted into each other. For example, the first and the last passages together form a textual unity, and the scheme is a classic account of a healing miracle (the nature of the illness, the healing and its affirmation).[1]

However another textual unity has been inserted into the story, and this is the argument between Jesus and some of the scribes. In all probability it reflects a disputation in *the early Christian Church*, which was then back-dated to Jesus's time by the evangelist. This does not imply that we cannot trace back the comforting words of forgiveness of sins to the historical Jesus, through whom God acts. But that this question was hotly discussed is shown by Mark integrating the *argument* about forgiving sins into the *healing miracle* through Jesus. "Your sins are forgiven you (by God)". The scribes understand Jesus to mean that he is forgiving sins in his own name and authority - "I forgive you your sins." But the whole weight of Jesus's words referring to the *healing miracle* lie in the connection between the *paralytic's sins* and his *illness*. On the other hand, the *dispute* which was slotted in by the evangelist is about *Jesus's divine authority* (who can forgive sins but God alone? The Son of Man!) This was a point of fierce dispute among the

170

first Judaeo-Christian communities. These circles sprang from Judaism and were still linked to it, and their insistent question was the one asked by the scribes in the story: "Who can forgive sins but God alone?" In Judaism not even the long-awaited Messiah had this authority. In dispute with this group, the early Church felt bound to prove that Jesus could lay legitimate claim to this prerogative because of his divine origin, and that for her part, the Church was empowered by Jesus to practice this authority. This is even clearer in Matthew's gospel than in Mark's. After the miracle Matthew says: "When the crowds saw it, they were afraid, and they glorified God, who had given such authority to men." (Mt 9,8). We can only give this statement its full weight if we remind ourselves that what is actually under discussion is nothing less than the Church's practice of forgiveness of sins. We shall return to this point later.

The miracle that provides a frame for the disputation also needs some explanation.

We are told that Jesus *comes back to Capernaum*, and *"that he was at home"*. Jesus has left Capernaum where he has healed Peter's mother-in-law (Mk 1,39), in order to spread his mission in Galilee. When the evangelist says that Jesus is at home, we assume that he is thinking of Peter's house. If we are talking about a house built like almost all the other houses in the district, it would have consisted of one large room. The roof would have been made of beams separated by reeds, hay and twigs woven together. The whole was then coated with clay and probably covered with boards, so that it formed a kind of roof terrace, where people could sit and talk, especially after sunset. The stairs were outside the house and led up to this roof. Many of these roofs had an opening that was usually left uncovered in summer; the corn and other foodstuffs lying in the sun to dry were then brought into the house through this opening.

A thick crowd pushes right up to the door towards Jesus as he is preaching before the house. The four men who want to bring the paralytic to Jesus are prevented from getting near him. They have the unusual idea of letting him down through the hole in the roof. This version of the story can probably be traced back to the evangelist, who would no longer have known the original reason for this odd behavior. The boundaries between medicine and magic were very fluid, so that in case of sickness, while people grasped at the known methods of healing, at the same time they would try to insure themselves against the influence of all kinds of demons carrying disease. It is therefore highly probable that in the original story, the sick man was lowered to Jesus, not because of the crowd, but to hoodwink the demon. It was important that it should not know where the main entrance to the house was, lest it might return! Of course it is possible that the evangelist knew about this, and chose to re-interpret the story because he disapproved of superstition.[2]

The sick man's bed which was carried on a stretcher would have been a rolled up mattress. These were spread out every evening on the floor of the house.

Sin - a "somewhat humorous word"

Every detailed commentary on the New Testament contains the factual comments we have been discussing. They help us find our way into the story. But in doing so, they do not clarify the evangelist's *point*.

As I have already said, Mark has theologically embellished the original story of the healing of the paralytic. His aim is to intervene in the topical dispute among the early Christian community about their claim to have the authority to forgive sins. However the original miracle story taken by the evangelist (without the disputation) is about the *connection between sin and disease.*

Linking sin and disease together may at first seem rather strange to us. But in fact the combination is not so unusual when we remind ourselves of what we today call psychosomatic illness. These are physical disturbances whose origins can be localized in the psychic area. It is not surprising when someone who has always been described as a loser gets an ulcer. He or she has always had to "swallow everything". Many dermatologists are convinced that skin rashes can often be traced back to people "not feeling at home in their own skins." Chronic insomnia and nightmares can also point to repressed experiences that have not been coped with. Our miracle story is concerned with these psychosomatic illnesses, with the difference that the psychic cause of the illness is called *sin.* We have to thank both Church propaganda and the priorities set by her moral teaching for the fact that, even in Church circles, the word "sin" is used as a signal. The Church does not leave us in peace, even in bed; everything we like either makes us fat or is a sin... In a letter to the writer Gerhard Hauptmann, Thomas Mann remarked succinctly that the concept of sin has been used as a "half good-natured, half familiar, and somewhat humorous word."[3]

In the New Testament sin always means removal from God and the self-deification of man. A pertinent example of this is the parable of the Prodigal Son (Lk 15,11-32). His sin is not that he disobeys rules or goes off with prostitutes, but that he turns away from his father. Without the imagery, this means that the actual point of reference to which man must orientate himself - God and his instruction given to man for his well-being - is replaced by idols according to which man lives his life. These idols are power, money, pleasure, physical beauty, career, or all of them put together. In that man selfishly furthers his own ends, he puts himself in God's place; he decides for himself what is good for him. According to biblical understanding, sin does not exist in the infringement of individual prohibitions or in violating specific rules or commandments. These misdemeanors do not constitute *the nature of sin* but are *a result of sin*, that is, the turning away from God, who has made man. In other words, what we generally describe as sins - the infringement of single commandments - have their roots in the breach with God, or in New Testament language, unbelief. This is the *very nature of sin* which then realizes itself in individual wrong-doings.

Therefore it should not surprise us that the account of the healing of the paralytic neither offers a diagnosis of his illness nor explains in detail in what way the sick man has erred. The causal link between sin and disease is of far more importance. The man is paralyzed because he is at the mercy of sin, or rather because *he has put himself* at the mercy of sin—his state has something to do with his freedom. His illness, seen biblically as his "unholiness", is not the result of individual misdemeanors but is conditioned by his perverted or *sinful* attitude towards life.

The primal link between sin and disease corresponds to the interaction between salvation and healing. Only when the paralytic has found his psychic equilibrium - his *soul's* healing - can he be healed of his *physical* disease. In order to re-discover his own peace he must find his way out of his ruined self and out of his estrangement from God. Or as the New Testament would put it, he must be freed from his sins. Exegetes are right to point out that the healings ascribed to Jesus are almost always the liberation of the sick person in himself and to God, and include the restoring of psychic equilibrium.[4]

Awakened to New Life

In the story of the healing of the paralytic, the facts are represented in a kind of time-lapse photography. "My son, your sins are forgiven you", and then almost immediately "Rise, take up your pallet and go home". In reality these events are about finding God and finding oneself and the healing involved, which as a rule is a process that extends over a length of time.

Leo Tolstoy describes this in masterly fashion and with convincing psychological insight in his novel "Resurrection".

There are two main characters in this book. One is Katuschka Maslova, the daughter of an unmarried girl who tends the cows. She is brought up by two aristocratic old ladies. The other is their nephew Prince Dimitri Nechludov, who seduces and then abandons her. After her child dies she ends up in a brothel. She is summoned to court, falsely accused of poisoning and robbing a freeman. As luck would have it her seducer is a member of the jury. He sees her for the first time after nine years. Although the jury find Katuschka innocent, the acquital is defective in form, and the girl is sent to Siberia to do four years forced labor.

As a landowner the Prince can afford every pleasure, but although he is constantly in search of new diversions, he is left unsatisfied. Somehow he has a feeling he is missing out on life. The court scene becomes a crucial experience for him; "In the depths of his soul he suddenly felt the vast cruelty and malice, not only of his deed, but the whole of his life, until now idle, easy-going, cruel, self-centered. And at last that terrible veil that had miraculously hidden his crimes and their consequences in his life for that long decade suddenly shifted, so that now here, now there he could glimpse behind it."[5]

175

Everything that Nechludov had formerly done amounted to nothing but self-deception. He desired only one thing after he had felt this disgust in life; he wanted at last "to breathe a little freely." To begin, he reflected that he had been quite a different person in his youth.

The difference between what he had been then and what he was now was immense; it was as great as, if not greater than the difference between Katushka in church and as the prostitute...they had condemned today...He remembered how he had once been proud of his uprightness, how he had made it a rule at the time to tell the truth always, and he had indeed been utterly truthful. Now he was enmeshed in a lie, in the most terrible of all lies, in a lie that everyone surrounding him took for the truth. And there was no escaping it, at least he saw no chance of it. He sank deeply into this lie, grew used to it, and nursed it.

In fact Nechludov is a prisoner or, what is almost the same thing, a paralytic. He knows he is guilty. If he had not seduced the inexperienced girl everything would have been different. Pricked by his conscience he determines to help her. He does not succeed in quashing the verdict in St Petersburg, so he follows her into exile in order to make her life a little easier. It takes some time before Nechludov realizes that he is only deceiving himself, and that the repugnance he feels for other people "is a repugnance for himself." In order to atone for his crime he decides to marry Katuschka. "I will tell her that I am a good-for-nothing and I will do everything I can to ameliorate her fate. Yes, I will see her and beg her to forgive me...I will marry her if necessary."

But once again these actions would have been merely self-deceptive. Nechludov imagines he is doing the right

176

thing, but in reality he is once more caught up in the frenzy of life with nothing to anchor him down, just as he had been when he seduced the girl and intended to "settle his folly with money." Katuschka refuses his proposal and forces him to confront himself at long last. For the first time he realizes that he is caught "in the net of his own stupid, empty, aimless and trivial life", and he sees "no way out of something from which he normally did not even want to escape."

He feels as if he were at the foot of a sheer cliff, and that every time he tries to climb up, the stones roll away from under his feet. But Katuschka is standing at the top on the edge, and her tender look gives him the feeling that she believes he will reach the top in the end, even if he sometimes loses his balance and slips back. And Katushka has time.

She has an intimation why he wants to marry her. For he has said to himself, "It is my duty to do what my conscience demands of me. It demands that I offer my freedom, so that I can atone for my sins. And my decision to marry her—even if the marriage is only on paper—and to follow her wherever she has to go, even into imprisonment, has not changed."

It is only during the course of time that Nechludov begins to understand that he cannot atone for his sin by linking his destiny with that of Katuschka, but by *radically* changing his "empty, aimless, and trivial life." This knowledge inspires him to make over his property to the peasants who are without means. He works to improve criminal law, and presses for necessary social reform. Once he has realized that man first of all "has to strive for the Kingdom of God", a new life begins for him, "not particularly because he had entered into an entirely different life, but because everything that had happened to him since had acquired an entirely new significance."

At the beginning of this chapter we asked ourselves how a person can find his way out of a state of inner paralysis and psychic apathy. It is only possible if we are helped. And this means we have to alter our question. How can we release someone from the state of despair and apathy into which he has manoeuvered himself through his behavior?

Katuschka will not marry Nechludov. But she forgives him for feigning love for her all those years ago, although he knew that the night they spent together would only remain a fleeting experience in his life. Katushka knows that guilt is part of life, and that one does not help someone by demanding reparation for it; this would make it a punishment, and not the expiation that contains the inner change within itself. And she sees that we may not push someone away who is making an effort to be strong enough to climb up the sheer cliff of his wasted life. Instead we must hold out a hand to him. This simple and most human of gestures expresses what Jesus says to the paralytic "Rise...and walk."

Rise and walk! Or we could put it like this: if we confine ourselves to buying freedom from our guilt by performing some action or other, we shall remain paralysed and become resigned to it. We can see only our mistakes and we find them acutely embarrassing, so that we forget to confront ourselves with the causes and motives that led us into this miserable situation. If we really want to be free and to stand up, we cannot have a fixation about our feelings of guilt. Instead we have to try to come to terms with the fact that we shall probably go on making wrong decisions (and probably suffer the consequences) all through life. But this does not make us criminals or damnable people.

It is part of being human that terrible things can happen to us, and that, sometimes precisely because of this, we can do terrible things to others. But it is also a part of our humanity that we are more than the sum of our mistakes and our guilt. And we have not yet fulfilled our humanity when we *pay off* our guilt, as Nechludov does at first. We can only become more human when we have questioned the reasons for and the background to our misdemeanors. Then we can lift ourselves up if someone says to us: "Rise, dare to try, and *go!*" Or: "Your guilt is forgiven you!"

The Fear of Accepting Yourself

Forgiveness. For centuries people have heard this word, not only from people they have offended, but also from the mouths of priests after they have confessed their sins. But even so, many of them never find the strength to rise up. They say their "penances" to pay off their guilt and go on hobbling through life on their miserable crutches. All this is quite understandable because it is not only individual sins and misdemeanors that lame us but the feeling that our penance has not achieved anything because it changes nothing. We are then further disabled by the constant (mostly unconscious) fear that we could do something else wrong on the very same day, and once again feel bitterly ashamed. This fear cannot be overcome by absolution from a priest. Absolution - not only in the confessional - can bring peace to our hearts only if it also helps us to accept ourselves, with all our mistakes, sins, and guilt. Above all else this is what God expects from us; not that we should be perfect but that we should accept ourselves.

The Church has frequently overlooked this and sometimes not even wanted to take it into account. Great stress has always been laid on perfection but far too little on acceptance, as if one could be realized without the other! This is an important reason why the sacrament of penance in the Church can lead down so many blind alleys.

To understand this we must remember that the history of the sacrament of confession is long and complicated. We know that the apostles did not sit in the confessional every

Saturday afternoon! At that time no one thought of "confession," because Jesus's *preaching* did not aim at re-conciliation—that is, a *second* changing of our ways—but at *changing* our ways. He invited us to believe in him and follow him.

However the *Church* soon discovered that some of the baptized became rather slack after their initial enthusiasm, and their behavior caused trouble. She tried to steer them in the opposite direction, towards the spirit of Christ. There is a famous example of this in Matthew's gospel, where he gives us some of the early community's rules (Mt 18,15-18). "If your brother sins against you, go and tell him his fault, between you and him alone." But if he does not listen to you, "take one or two others along with you..." And if he still refuses to listen, "tell it to the Church" (the community). If the sinner still remains obstinate the community shall excommunicate him, that is, banish him from their midst.

Sometime later there was discussion about a "second remission of sins" for those who had faulted after baptism, which wiped out all sin and was then administered almost entirely to adults. Finally the community came to the conclusion that serious offenses, like murder, adultery (when known), serious theft or a falling off of belief could be forgiven but not through baptism which is God's pure act of grace. Difficult penitential works corresponding to the offenses would have to be performed. The guilty made their offenses known to the bishop and were then admitted into the "penitential state", which meant they could not receive Holy Communion, sometimes had to practice fasting and were frequently told to abstain from physical intimacy in marriage. As a rule reconciliation and re-admittance to the Church took place on Maundy Thursday.

This "second changing of ways" was only permitted once. In order to avoid the results of a possible lapse and the harsh penances demanded before re-acceptance into the community, it became customary to plead for the penitential state to be delayed until old age or even until the deathbed. In 538 the Church Synod in Orléans forbade young and already married members of the faithful to be admitted to confession because of the unrealistic obligations attached to it!

In the 6th century, abbots in Irish and Anglo-Saxon monasteries began to admit the faithful to confession and reconciliation. Not only the bishop, but the ordinary priest could pronounce the words of forgiveness in the name of the Church *before* the faithful had to fulfill the still harsh penitential practices, which were written down in so-called "Penitential Books". The following short extract comes from one of these. Some scholars ascribe it to the English monk Bede (d. 735).

He who drinks until he has to vomit must fast for forty days if he is a priest or a deacon: if a lay brother, for thirty days, and for twelve days if he is a lay man. He who vomits because he is ill does not sin. He who vomits because he has eaten too much shall fast for three days. He who gets drunk in spite of his master's orders, but does not vomit afterwards, shall fast for seven days.

An unmarried man who has a sinful relationship with another man's wife must fast for two years. A married man who has a sinful relationship with a married woman must fast for three years. During the first year he may not approach his own wife. (Fasting meant abstaining from numerous dishes, and living on bread, water, vegetables and fruit, which were permitted.)[6]

Strict obedience of this "penitential rate" (this was the unfriendly term) was almost beyond endurance and posed a hindrance to reconciliation with God and the Church, so a remedy was devised. For example, people could work off a long fast through prayer and alms giving, through supporting good works for the community or through Masses. Or they could find someone else to work it off for them. This was the origin of indulgences.

The teaching instructions of the Council of Trent (1551) were important in the further development of the sacrament of confession. There is no more mention of public confession in church, but only of auricular private confession. All mortal sins had to be confessed, how many times they had been committed, and their circumstances. This meant that confession was a sort of tribunal, and the priest functioned as a judge.

Even this brief summary shows that the crisis today about confession in the Church has some of its origins in the fact that, to a large extent, the Church has allowed herself to be ruled by dogmatic criteria when considering the sacrament of reconciliation. Of necessity, this has contributed to inhumane development. Indeed we miss almost all of the psychological understanding that shines through the brotherly rebuke in the rules of the community (Mt. 18,15-18) quoted previously. The tribunal is no longer only a *model* for confession. Confession *turns into* a tribunal. And it would have been possible to find more suitable models in the New Testament. We only have to remember the meeting of Jesus and the tax collector Zacchaeus (Lk 19,1-10). Jesus utters not one word of judgement. Or we can again remind ourselves of the parable of the Prodigal Son (Lk 15,11-32) where the father spares his son all reproach.

These impressive stories are in direct contrast to the dogmatic jungle of teaching on the sacrament of confession since the Council of Trent. The points of discussion are numerous: whether the priest acts as a judge, whether imperfect remorse is enough to obtain absolution, and why perfect remorse is better; why one is made to mention the different or varied circumstances of a mortal sin; who has the right to hear confession; how often should one go to confession...

Naturally we have to see these statements in their historical context before we can judge them. But even if our observations are based on how these rules came into being historically, it does not alter the fact that these dogmatic decisions disguise pastoral helplessness, and in practice this is often covered up by empty phrases and hackneyed, meaningless sentences like "we want to include everything..."

When a person is paralysed by guilt and seeks forgiveness we have no right to judge him, but simply to understand. If the father had overwhelmed his prodigal son with reproaches, the son would not have been able to take one more step towards him or stammer out another syllable to beg him for forgiveness; he would have stood there paralysed and then collapsed completely.

Once we have recognized our guilt we need to try to make reparation for the evil we have caused. We do not have to be told this. But perhaps we should realize that this is not the main problem.

Certainly Jesus says to the paralytic "Rise!" But he adds *"Take up your pallet* and go home." This can only mean: this pallet you have been lying on belongs to you. You must not repress your past. Only when you are capable of acknowledging this past will you be able to walk upright. Say "Yes" to yourself, then you will feel new life within you, in a way that only lovers feel, as if spring had suddenly burst upon your heart.

8

Standing on your own Feet

The Raising of the Widow's Son in Nain
(Lk 7,11-17)

Without exception all men strive to be happy, however varied the paths they take may be. All have this goal. The same desire, however multifarious, lives within us all, and moves some men to go to war and others not to go to war. The will cannot be moved to any action, for all seek happiness. This is the reason for every action in all men, even those who are on the point of hanging themselves.[1]

The French philosopher Blaise Pascal (1623-1662) is right to a certain extent. What else do we search for all our lives except escape from all unhappiness, protection from pain, and freedom from fear? We do not even make the sacrifices we believe we should make; we always make them for the sake of something worthwhile. We all want to develop and realize ourselves - to be happy, to live.

And yet our lives are constantly threatened by death. This is not only because we search obstinately and blindly for happiness in the wrong place, but because death itself sets boundaries to our existence that we do not want to acknowledge or be aware of - we repress them only too gladly.

But time after time we are confronted by death's boundaries, not only biologically, but in its "temporary" form of appearance in suffering, in physical pain or some blow of fate, or in sorrow, leading to deep depression or blank

184

despair.

An episode from the life of Apollonius, one of the best known miracle workers in the ancient world, illustrates how we are not only faced with death at every moment of our lives, but also with all the possible forces of death in its threatening harbingers. Apollonius was a contemporary of Paul who came from Tyana, a town in the Roman province of Cappadocia in Asia Minor. Philostratos, a writer at the court of the Roman Emperor Septimus Severus, witnessed the following scene. About the year 200 AD he wrote a biography of Apollonius.

A girl, on the point of marrying, seemed to be dead, and the bridegroom followed her bier. He was lamenting the early death of his bride, and all Rome mourned with him, for the girl was a member of a consul's family. Apollonius came up just at that moment and heard about the sorrow. He said; "Set down the bier. I will wipe away the tears you are weeping over this girl." Then he asked her name. The people thought he wanted to make a speech as was customary at a funeral to assuage their grief. But instead he just touched the girl and whispered something to her. He woke her from seeming death. And the girl spoke and went into her father's house... Her relations wanted to give Apollonius 150,000 sestercii. But he wished them to use it for the girl's dowry.

Whether he had found a flicker of life still within her that the doctors had not noticed, or whether her life was really extinguished and he had brought it back through the warmth of his touch is an exceedingly difficult question that neither I nor those present could answer.[2]

The Course of Life and the Procession of Death.

This story reminds us in some ways of an episode in the New Testament which has only been handed down by Luke. In it he describes how the course of life and the procession of death suddenly come together.

Soon afterwards he (Jesus) went to a city called Nain, and his disciples and a great crowd went with him. As he drew near the gate of the city, behold, a man who had died was being carried out, the only son of his mother, and she was a widow, and a large crowd from the city was with her. And when the Lord saw her he had compassion on her and said to her, "Do not weep." And then he came and touched the bier, and the bearers stood still. And he said, "Young man, I say to you, arise." And the dead man sat up, and began to speak. And he gave him to his mother. Fear seized them all; and they glorified God, saying "A great prophet has arisen among us!" And this report concerning him spread through the whole of Judea and all the surrounding country. (Lk 7,11-17).

As Jesus and his disciples—not only the apostles but a large group of followers (Lk 6,13-17)—were going towards Jerusalem they came upon a funeral procession in the town of Nain. This little town in South Galilee is called Nen today and has about 200 Muslim inhabitants. At Jesus's time it was an unimportant hamlet. It seems that Luke, who wrote his gospel between 85 and 90 AD, probably in Greece or Asia Minor, did not know the place himself. It is not surprising that he imagines it as a Hellenic city, surrounded by a wall.

There are many *differences* between Luke's account and that of Philostratos—a young man, a girl—awakening

186

through touching the bier or touching the dead person—following the stories of raising from the dead in the Hebrew Bible, allusions to Greek mythology—the witnesses' glorification of Jesus, the narrator's attempt to explain. On the other hand certain *similarities* catch the eye: both miracle workers meet up with a funeral procession, one of the mourners is closely connected with the dead person, the healer comforts them, and finally brings about the miracle.

Naturally it would have been impossible for Luke to have used Philostratos because his account was written more than a century after the gospel. But we should not forget that *the motif of a divinity raising the dead* is far older than Christianity. This explains why Philostratos's miracle story is constructed in much the same way as Luke's. The likeness between the two is primarily of a formal kind.

However Luke's gospel has many similarities with another miracle story which happened quite near Nain. This part of the world is mentioned nowhere else in the Bible, but it lies in the neighborhood of Shunem, where the prophet Elisha, disciple and follower of Elijah, awakened a dead child to life (2 Kings 4,18-37). The naming of the place indicates a link between the two accounts. But a direct dependence is improbable. On the other hand, we know that Elisha's miracle refers back to another story. Tradition has it that Elisha's disciples had "modified" a miracle on the same subject done by Elijah and attributed it to their master. They wanted to prove that Elisha was no less powerful than his predecessor and teacher Elijah.

Luke would have known both accounts. But the orientation for his story was the awakening of the dead attributed to Elijah. A comparison makes this quite clear.[3]

At God's command Elijah goes to Zarephath, a town on the coast south of Sidon.

*So he arose and went to Zarephath; when he came to the
gate of the city, behold, a widow was there gathering sticks...*

*After this the son of the woman, the mistress of the house,
became ill; and his illness was so severe that there was no
breath in him.*

*And she said to Elijah "What have you against me, O man
of God? You have come to me to bring my sin to remem-
brance, and to cause the death of my son! " And he said to
her "Give me your son!" And he took him from her bosom,
and carried him up to the upper chamber, where he lodged,
and laid him on his bed. And he cried to the Lord, "O Lord,
my God, hast thou brought calamity even upon the widow
with whom I sojourn, by slaying her son?" Then he stretched
himself upon the child three times and cried to the Lord "O
Lord, my God, let this child's soul come into him again!"*

*The Lord hearkened to the voice of Elijah; and the soul of
the child came into him again, and he revived. Elijah took
the child, and brought him down from the upper chamber
into the house, and delivered him to his mother; and Elijah
said "See, your son lives." And the woman said to Elijah,
"Now I know that you are a man of God, and that the word
of the Lord in your mouth is truth." (1 Kings 17,10f;17-24).*

The similarities between the miracles at Zarephath and Nain
are striking. Both accounts are written in Greek and begin
with the same word (*égeneto:* he made his way, he went).
The miracle workers' first meeting with the mothers takes
place before the gates of the city. In both cases the dead are
the only sons of widows. And both sons have just died. In
the first story the boy has hardly emitted his last breath when
the prophet goes to him. It is the same with Jesus, for at the
time the dead were simply covered with a winding sheet, laid
on a bier and buried on the same day outside the town. In
both stories the miracle workers give their sons back to their

mothers and are praised as the man of God (Elijah) and a great prophet (Jesus).

In view of the similarities of form and content we may conclude that Luke was thinking of the Elijah miracle when he wrote down his story. But on the other hand, there are such important differences that we cannot just assume that Luke *was the only person* to use this story as orientation or simply copy it.

In contrast to Elijah Jesus is not *addressed* by the weeping mother, *he* turns towards *her*. Whilst the prophet *asks Yahweh* to awaken the dead and is heard by him, according to the evangelist Jesus already has this strength *in him*; he awakens the boy with a powerful word (and does not even touch him, only the bier). Elijah is described by the widow as a man of God who proclaims the word of the Lord. Jesus appears as a great prophet in whom *God himself* comes towards his people.

Factual Report or narrative Theology?

Do we then infer that Luke's story of the raising of the dead in Nain is not describing a historical event but merely saying that Jesus, as Lord of life *and* death, will give life to all those who follow him? (Jn 11,25)

From a historical point of view it is fair to ask whether this miracle has been handed down as fact, or whether it is dealing with theological doctrine in narrative form. We are not discussing the *possibility* of raising the dead, but simply asking whether we can maintain that Jesus did indeed awaken the dead to life. We have already established that accounts of raising the dead were not unknown in the ancient world, and that the Hebrew Bible reports them. According to the tradition passed down in the Talmud, some rabbis also performed this miracle. [4]

Jesus is credited with three raisings from the dead in the New Testament; the raising of the daughter of Jairus (Mk 5,22-24, 35-43; Mt 9,18-19, 23-26; Lk 8,40-42,49-56); the young man in Nain (Lk 7,11-17) and Lazarus (Jn 11,1-44). For various reasons it is not possible to pass final judgement on whether these three accounts are founded on historical truth. Firstly there is the fact that the concept "dead" had many meanings in the languages of the time. Sick people, for whom there was no hope of healing were called "the dead." And it was often said of people who were rescued from danger of death that they had been called back from death into life (Ps 55,5-19; 88,6).

Added to this, the biblical descriptions of raisings from the dead had been through various stages as they were handed down, so that at best the original story can still be reconstructed, but not the basic facts. According to Mark, Jairus calls Jesus to him because his daughter is ill (Mk 5,23). Through meeting the woman with an issue of blood (an episode that was certainly added later), Jesus is delayed on his way to the house of Jairus, the ruler of the synagogue. When he arrives there the girl has just died. In contrast, Matthew, who used Mark's gospel as his model, intensifies the story; Jesus is called when the girl is already dead (Mt 9,18).

As far as the raising of Lazarus is concerned, according to John's gospel, the decisive factor is that the Council decides that Jesus must be killed (Jn 11,45-53). The other three evangelists know nothing about this, nor do they mention the raising of Lazarus, which in John's eyes is the most sensational of Jesus's miracles. Besides, John's reason for proclaiming it seems almost too clear. For example, Jesus delays his arrival in Bethany on purpose, so that he can reveal his power through a miracle (11,6-15). Only one thing is certain in this story, and that is the evangelist's desire to draw his

190

readers' attention to the statement that Jesus is "the resurrection and the life" (11,25). It is essential that people should believe *this*, not whether they believe or do not believe in his raising the dead. The latter is anyway not a question of belief, but of history. And because of the source, and above all because of the nature of this gospel's narrative, this question can only be one of conjecture.

Of course this is also true of the miracle of Nain which comes from a tradition only known to Luke. And he was not simply concerned to describe a spectacular event. In depicting he also proclaims. Above all he wants to show us who Jesus is. However he does not do this through abstract formulae of faith as the great Councils of the Church did later, but by means of story-telling. In that he speaks of Jesus as *Lord* (7,13: "And when the Lord saw her, he had compassion on her") he underlines his divinity. In the Greek translation of the Hebrew Bible God's name is given as *kyrios* (Lord). As a result, the New Testament authors use this title whenever they want to emphasize Jesus's divine origin.

And the whole story of the raising of the widow's son in Nain amounts to this. Luke is not concerned to prove that Jesus is greater than Elijah; his aim is to illustrate through the story that *God's life-giving strength itself works in Jesus.*

But Luke is not content with this alone. At the same time he points to the fact that professing Jesus as the *Lord* has practical consequences: Jesus here sets an example of how those who call upon him should behave. Like the Lord they should have compassion.

Compassion is something that lies very close to Luke's heart. Unlike any of the other evangelists, Jesus's compassion and mercy lie at the center of his gospel. He alone tells us how Jesus wept over his city, full of grief and sorrow that she was beyond help because she had rejected his message (19,41f). And it is only in Luke that we find the moving

191

accounts of the Lost Drachma and the Prodigal Son (15,8-32), the comforting story of Jesus's meeting with the woman, a sinner, who anoints his feet with ointment (7,36-50), and the tax collector Zacchaeus. The last two remind us that the experience of mercy and compassion can become a perfect example of blessedness.

"The Lord had compassion on her." Jesus's compassion was not only for the pain the widow suffers over the loss of her son. He was also thinking of the unhappy lot that awaited her, because a widow whose only son died also lost her support for her old age. Such a woman was a human being without hope, without a future. From now on she would be the property of her dead husband's family, and tolerated as a servant. She was without protection, without anyone to represent her interests in a society in which only men had a say. This situation had already been denounced by the prophets who frequently raised their voices against the injustices that were practiced against widows and orphans: "Correct oppression; defend the fatherless, plead for the widow." (Is 1,17)

Arise!

Out of compassion for this woman and her bitter lot Jesus takes the law into his own hands. He touches the bier, he orders the dead boy to get up and gives him back to his mother.

"Arise!" Although he says this to the son, the widow he has just told not to weep anymore is also included; she who is bowed down with sorrow and pain, shall also arise.

We have already indicated the moral that Luke points to in this story. Jesus's followers are called upon to follow his example. That leaves us with "the remains of the story", and following the evangelist's intentions, this must be interpreted according to the situation.

More than ever before, present day psychology emphasizes the fundamental significance of the mother-son relationship, and the effect it can have on the future life of the son. Most of us know something about the mistakes and pathological disturbances that can occur in this relationship. Without reference to any psychological theories or patterns of behavior Luke's story shows that this relationship is the embodiment of the close (or the closest) common bond which also affects the future. The son is his mother's only property and there are specific expectations and anxieties attached to this, particularly those related to care in old age.[5]

A woman who has lost her husband early tends to place all her hopes on her only son, not only for material reasons, but out of a sense of loneliness and emptiness. It is easy to imagine such a woman giving everything, including herself, to promote her son's development and happiness without noticing that her tireless care and secret anxieties constrict his life.

Of course the same thing can be said of fathers!

Parents can work themselves into a state of exhaustion trying to give their sons and daughters what they never had, so that their children can live as they were never able to do themselves. This excessive care is not free of unacknowledged and unconscious self-interest, and can give rise to tragedies that turn children into psychological cripples. These children have been brought up to be entirely dependent, and this manifests itself sooner or later in career failure, broken relationships, social isolation, and finally in illnesses that are the physical symptoms of psychological suffering. In the end these are the result of excessive so-called love, which under closer examination is seen to blackmail and bleed people white.

It is understandable that the suffering of the son, unconsciously and not willingly caused by the mother, comes from her own pain. The sicknesses feed and condition each other. "Do not weep". If we transfer these words to the *above* situation they mean: it is time you understood that your existence is not dependent on the kind of life you have sketched out for your son. Let him finally escape from under the shadow you have spread around him and over him with your advice, which is really no more than making demands on him, and your protectiveness, which comes from the egoism you will not acknowledge. Do not weep! Let your son go free, let him *live at last!*

Jesus's command is not softened by any other words of comfort. Admittedly it sounds hard. But it springs from his compassion. And are there not situations where compassionate help must sound hard so that it does not just become a verbose putting off of the truth? It is necessary to open someone's eyes if their unhappiness is grounded in their own behavior, even if this causes excruciating pain at first.

In this case however, the son needs help as well as the mother. Again Jesus does not say much, but according to the original Greek text, confines himself to one word in the form of a command: "Arise!" In other words, you do not have to have a guilty conscience if you do not respond any longer to your mother's secretive attempts at blackmail, and finally make up your mind to live according to your *own* ideas, to realize *your* dreams, stand up for *your* own longings, briefly, find the courage to live your *own* life. Of course your mother will suffer at first. The process of letting go will be very difficult for her, but you must both go through it. If she feels how self-sufficient and happy you are that you have managed to free yourself from her and lead your own life, she will gradually understand that she can certainly go on looking after you but not in a way that makes you feel guilty all the time so that you cannot breathe.

This is the freedom that parents must allow their children without following every step with over-anxious care and seeing every false step as a tragedy. If you bind a person to you, you have lost him, robbed him of his freedom and his space to move in, and thus of his life.

Psychological mechanisms of this kind do not only happen between parents and children, but in every human relationship. We only have to remind ourselves of the bare fact that we tend to limit other people's freedom by having certain expectations of them, and letting them know this. To a large extent this is because we have created an image of them. We make claims because we think we know people. We have a specific idea of them, and this idea is what we approve of or reject. And of course we expect them to correspond to our image; we claim it as our right.

"You shall not make for yourself a graven image" (Ex 20,4). The novelist Max Frisch applies this quotation both to God and man many times. In fact it happens so often in relationships that we do not love a person but the image we have made of him or her. In his novel "Stiller" Max Frisch illustrates how this inevitably leads to disaster. Stiller is an unsuccessful sculptor who believes he loves his wife. Julika is a ballet dancer, and her career means more to her, or at least not less, than her marriage. Stiller believes it is his task to give this woman life and joy. He has "put her on probation".[6] But the relationship does not fail because Stiller thinks he can win his wife for himself away from her art, but because he does not love Julika the person, only the image he has created of her. At least this is how she sees it when she reproaches him:

"You only once made a sculpture of me, and I noticed it was a complete and final image, and that was it. I feel you don't want to see me as anything else. Isn't that true?" Stiller lit

195

a cigarette. "I've thought over a lot of things recently" said Julika... "it's not for nothing that in the commandments it says 'You shall not make for yourself a graven image.' Every image is a sin. It's exactly the opposite of love... I don't know if you understand. If you love another person, you have to leave every moment open to him, and in spite of all memories of him you must simply be ready to be amazed at how different he is, how diverse, and not simply just so, not a finished image like the one you want to make of your Julika. I can only say it's not like that. You always meddle - but you should not make an image...that's all I can say."

If you make images of other people you can never build up a true relationship with them. You either reject or accept them because of some characteristic you have credited them with, that they may not even possess. If the image is negative there is no contact. If it is positive it is no more than a projection of your own affirmative concept of them, and the relationship cannot grow. Sooner or later it will be succeeded by disappointment. To the extent that the (ideal) concept does not tally with reality, people usually react by withdrawing love, as Stiller does. And as soon as a partner feels that love and devotion are not directed towards him but towards an image, he experiences loneliness because he realizes that he has always been misunderstood, and never approved of as the person he really is. He has just lived for a time with the illusion that he had met someone who understands him. The disappointment is then mutual. It is no accident that Stiller discovers he is a failure when one of the other characters in the novel says of Julika: "I think I have never seen a person more lonely than this woman."

Stiller has failed; he felt himself called to redeem his wife, but he has become her death, because he did not let her live. He is like the widow who follows her son's bier after causing his death.

We can only get out of these blind alleys and find our way back to the other person if both parties are willing to make their contribution, and this is intimated in the story of the raising of the young man by Jesus *challenging* both the widow and her dead son: "Do not weep!" and "Arise!"

But are these psychological interpretations not rather far fetched? Do they really correspond to the evangelist's intention? It is clear that we shall miss the point of the gospel if we scale it down to psychological or anthropological facts. But it is also clear that we make it into an ideology if we think we can detach it from all human experience.

The *whole* of Jesus's proclamation reminds us of how man is capable of taking the step from death to life. It shows us what life is, and that this life can only unfold and flourish in the space of responsible freedom. Neither parental expectations nor social norms nor current conventions can be the standards that finally bind us as beneficial for life and therefore for personal fulfillment.

This thought is the basis of the story of the young man from Nain. It also says expressly that God has visited his people in Jesus's actions (Luke 7,16). Besides, the story tells us how not one person, but two, are raised from the dead.

9

Rejected, Excluded, Banished

The Healing of the Ten Lepers (Lk 17,11-19)

Nothing hurts as much as thanklessness, and we know, this is the world's reward. It may be a reason why the account of Jesus's healing of the ten lepers was so misunderstood by exegetes in the early centuries and later by popular proclaimers of the gospel as a moral tale about the virtue of gratitude.

On the way to Jerusalem he (Jesus) was passing along between Samaria and Galilee. And as he entered a village, he was met by ten lepers, who stood at a distance and lifted up their voices and said, "Jesus, Master, have mercy on us." When he saw them he said to them, "Go and show yourselves to the priests." And as they went they were cleansed. Then one of them, when he saw that he was healed, turned back, praising God with a loud voice; and he fell on his face at Jesus's feet, giving him thanks. Now he was a Samaritan. Then said Jesus, "Were not ten cleansed? Where are the nine? Was no one found to return and give praises to God except this foreigner?" And he said to him "Rise and go your way; your faith has made you well" (Lk 17,11-19).

Before we try to understand the point the evangelist is making in this story, it is worth considering how the story of the lepers actually found its way into Luke's gospel. He

198

is the only evangelist to hand it down. Presumably it was an embellishment of another episode, the healing of one leper, which is found in all three synoptic gospels. Mark, who was Luke's model, tells the story thus:

And a leper came to him, beseeching him, and kneeling said to him; "If you will, you can make me clean." Moved with pity, he stretched out his hand and touched him, and said to him, "I will; be clean." And immediately the leprosy left him, and he was made clean. And he sternly charged him, and sent him away at once, and said to him; "See that you say nothing to anyone; but go, show yourself to the priest, and offer for your cleansing what Moses commanded, for a proof to the people" (Mk 1,40-44; Mt 8,1-4; Lk 5,12-14).

Not History but Catechesis

The link between the two stories lies in Jesus's almost identical command to go and show yourself to the priest or priests.[1] Also the *first* part of the story about the ten has the same structure as Mark's account. Everything indicates that Luke (or tradition before him?) enlarged or re-shaped the latter. This kind of embellishment or intensification of traditions can be attributed to the fact that many of them were handed down by word of mouth, and the Christian preachers would sometimes lay more emphasis on one motif, some-times on another, depending on the circumstances at the time. We can see this phenomenon in the gospels themselves. In Matthew two blind men are healed (9,27-31), and this story is a re-shaping of the healing of blind Bartimaeus in Mark (10,46-52). Mark only refers to one demoniac in Gerasa (5,1-20) while Matthew mentions two (8,28-34).[2]

The number ten (lepers) simply stands for "many", and

later serves the necessary subtraction of one from the remaining nine. There are good reasons to assume that Luke's story of the ten lepers represents a re-working of Mark's account.

But it is not only this. Some elements of the text go even further back to the Hebrew Bible, or more exactly to the story of Naaman, the commander of the Syrian army, who was a leper (2 Kings 5,1-19). He is in the service of the King of Aram, and by chance he hears from a girl who has been abducted from Israel that there is a prophet with extraordinary powers in that land who could heal him. The prophet is Elisha. The commander decides to look for him.

So Naaman came with his horses and chariots, and halted at the door of Elisha's house. And Elisha sent a messenger to him, saying, "Go and wash in the Jordan seven times, and your flesh shall be restored, and you shall be clean." But Naaman was angry, and went away, saying, "Behold, I thought that he would surely come out to me, and stand, and call on the name of the Lord, his God, and wave his hand over the place, and cure the leper. Are not...the rivers of Damascus better than all the waters of Israel? Could I not wash in them, and be clean?" So he turned and went away in rage. But his servant came near and said to him, "My father, if the prophet had commanded of you to do some great thing, would you not have done it? How much rather, then, when he says to you 'Wash and be clean?' " So he went down and dipped himself seven times in the Jordan, according to the word of the man of God; and his flesh was restored like the flesh of a little child, and he was clean.

Then he returned to the man of God, he and all his company, and he came, and stood before him; and he said, "Behold, I know that there is no God in all the earth but in Israel; so accept now a present from your servant." But he said, "As

the Lord lives, whom I serve, I will receive none." And he
urged him to take it, but he refused (2 Kings 5,9-16).

As in the story of the ten lepers, the man is sent away, and
the miracle happens *from a distance.* Like the one leper out
of the ten, Naaman *returns* to the prophet, to *thank* him. And
in both cases, thanks is given to *God.* In both stories the man
honored by God is a stranger.

These parallels are so striking that we can assume Luke
took his story from Mark, but was also influenced by the
account of Naaman and Elisha. And this assumption can be
substantiated by the use of words. The evangelist would have
had the Greek translation of Naaman's story to hand, and his
own text, also written in Greek, bears many verbal resem-
blances to it.[3]

If Luke's depiction is so strongly influenced by both Mark's
gospel and the miracle story from the chronicles of Elisha,
we can probably assume that he was not dealing with a
historical event, but handing down theological instructions.
It is striking how he shows not the slightest interest in details
that would have been significant to historians. For instance,
the place where everything happened is only mentioned
vaguely as the border between Samaria and Galilee. We are
told that Jesus is on his way to Jerusalem from his own
country. Obviously Luke, whose home was probably Greece
or Asia Minor, was not familiar with these districts, as he
mentions them the wrong way round when describing this
journey. The lepers are also surprisingly anonymous, and
we learn nothing about their past or future. The evangelist
is silent about how they are able to recognize Jesus, and
where he heals them along the road. And whether they
actually go to the priests afterwards, as Jesus has commanded
them, is also left open. This command, taken from Mark's
text (1,44) about the healing of one leper, refers to the law
about lepers in the 14th chapter of Leviticus, which is almost

entirely composed of legal instructions. If a leper was healed of his disease he had first of all to convince a priest of his cure, and then the priest would undertake the cleansing ritual which involved sacrificial offerings. Only after a man had presented these offerings was he deemed clean. Although anyone could confirm the disease or its cure, the *verdict* of clean or unclean had to come from the priest.

Lepers were excluded from the community even though it was probably known by Jesus's time that the disease was not infectious. Their exclusion was not the result of medical consideration but for the sake of the people's sacredness - they saw themselves particularly threatened by the uncleanliness of leprosy. According to rabbinical opinion, a leper made everything (ritually) unclean, not only what he touched. His entering a house, according to some rabbis, made everything found within unclean "to the height of four ells" or "to the height of the beams".[4] Lepers were therefore made "to dwell alone" (Lev 13,46) which meant not with other people who were "unclean" because of their profession, such as butchers, tanners, grave diggers or tax collectors. In a few cases it might have been true that lepers had to live outside the town walls in leper colonies especially prepared for them, but there is no evidence that this was a general custom. However there is no doubt that the leper's fate was terrible. When the ten lepers called out to Jesus "at a distance", this description corresponded to the current laws: "the leper who has the disease shall wear torn clothes and let the hair of his head hang loose, he shall cover his upper lip and cry 'unclean' " (Lev 13,45). And he had to keep his distance from ordinary people. Meeting a leper by chance could make a person unclean, and even a leper sitting down in a particular place made those present unclean. "If an unclean person sits under a tree and a clean man stands, he will become unclean. If a clean person sits under a tree and the unclean man stands, the clean person remains clean, but if the unclean man sits down, the clean man becomes unclean."[5]

If you were unable to find your way through these subtle directions - and this implied the vast majority of Jesus's fellow countrymen who were mostly uneducated - you simply avoided lepers, even when you saw them from a great distance. The leper was not only despised and rejected, he was excluded and expelled from society.

Lepers in Our Time

Perhaps we can only begin to understand this terrible state of affairs if we are able to put ourselves in the position of the many people *today* who live outside normality, or outside that which we *describe* as normal in a society or church and who not only orientate themselves towards the laws in force but also towards conventions that may be unwritten, and therefore all the more firmly entrenched in us. *Other* people are treated as contemptuous and lawless because they go their own way, often precisely because they are forced to, otherwise they would have to give up.

A woman leaves her husband after many years of marriage because she feels their relationship has never been real, although they had both a church and civil ceremony. It was never "consummated", in the sense that the partners never got close together but remained strangers, and to a certain extent, treated each other as strangers. Now and again they were able to look into each other's eyes, but never with affection. In short, this woman one could describe as "once bitten twice shy." Because she really knows what hell is like, she leaves her husband, not for any ulterior motive, but simply because she cannot breathe.

After this she is ignored by most of her friends. She is less than welcome in the social circles she frequented earlier - and what savage irony - because her husband's position demanded it. Her best friend will have nothing more to do with her, and other friends pretend they do not know her. One or two acquaintances behave a little more discreetly - although they distance themselves a bit and no longer visit her in her new apartment. There is no one she can talk to about her situation, and when she writes to people, the replies, if any, are now brief and impersonal.

Or there is a priest who has *failed* not because of celibacy, but who, after long struggles with God and with himself, realizes that although he may be suited to the priesthood, he is not suited to living alone. And because this burden is so heavy his spiritual vocation becomes more and more difficult, and he decides to take the inevitable step and resign his position in the Church. But he has not reckoned with the reaction of some of his colleagues. They refuse to have any more contact with him. They are not interested in his personal problems and give him to understand that although they are priests who are there to administer pastoral care, they are not there for priests who opt out. But our priest is even more deeply hurt by the reaction of some individuals active within the parish. Certain women who adored him as a second Messiah now speak badly about him, as if he had personally robbed them of something by leaving. The most pious among the pious voice their opinions on the telephone or send anonymous letters in envelopes addressed to "the drop-out priest", so that even the postman knows he is delivering letters to a monster.

Of course these are exceptional situations. Day to day life is usually far more mundane, but not less dramatic. People who do not know what you expect from them, who are somehow "different" and behave in a conspicuous way or disregard generally accepted customs (because they have to?) are very soon made aware of what society thinks of them. They are given to understand and often in an extremely brutal way that their role as an "outsider" is not acceptable. In that they *think* that they isolate themselves, we isolate them.

There are many ways of forcing people into the outsider's role, of turning them into pariahs and treating them like lepers. How can they be helped, and how can they help themselves?

This is the first question that is answered in the story of the healing of the ten lepers. Although everyone avoids them, Jesus shows no prejudice towards them, on the contrary, he gives them his full attention and listens to their misery. In Mark's text, which this story partly refers to, it is expressly said that Jesus suffers with the leper (in Greek *splagchnistheis*, which means having pity on someone). For this reason, he is not afraid to touch the man: "Moved with pity, he stretched out his hand and touched him, and said to him 'I will; be clean'" (Mk 1,41). Here the evangelist gives his readers an example of how they can help people out of their isolation and bitterness. To *help* them out, not to *bring* them out! Solicitous thinking, a charitable attitude and sending signals of care and understanding alone do not give an "outsider" a new perspective. The support that he gets from others is no more or less than first aid. Experienced sympathy from others can and should motivate him to take his fate into his own hands, and so advance the process of healing.

Luke's story expresses this in Jesus sending the lepers to the priests, for they are the judges who decide what is clean and unclean. "Go and show yourselves to the priests" (Lk 17,14).

In one short sentence Luke summarizes what happens in every day life in slow motion, according to both the afflicted

205

person and the psychotherapist. "Words of this nature, transferred into our life, must be repeated so often, and so patiently conveyed that they often require years of inner attention before they become credible. For all human experience speaks against wanting to do and being able to do what is so immense, so dreadful."[6]

Someone inwardly destroyed by his disturbance lives in isolation from society, and has need of immense energy before he can look other people in the face again openly, and be conscious of his own dignity. Although he *feels* himself afflicted with all the signs of "leprosy" nevertheless he has to have the courage to face others, to expose himself to the judge's glance in political meetings and church and social events. So that the theological statement in our story can have some bearing upon the reality of everyday life, I quote again from the psychotherapist Eugen Drewermann: "If it becomes clear that people can only regain health if they dare to penetrate normality as they are, then it is clear that the whole of 'normal' life must be changed. It must become more open-hearted, more understanding, compassionate and humane. It must be capable of grasping the deep, underground interconnections of human nature. Only then can we speak of healing".[7]

Eugen Drewermann's thoughts are echoed in verse form by Kurt Marti in his poem "Leichenreden." He asks whether the iron laws that people use to organize and single out others do not create the problem that they pretend to solve.[8]

We mourn for this man
not because he has died
we mourn for this man
because he never dared
to be happy

we mourn for this man
who was only work and duty
we mourn for this man
because he always did
what was demanded of him

we mourn for this man
who never banged his fist on the table
we mourn for this man
because he never cocked a snook
at other people's judgements
or did what he wanted to do

we mourn for this man
who functioned without a mistake
we mourn for this man
because he avoided strife and women
and is praised by all today

we mourn for this man
not because he is dead
we mourn for this man
because he was as we are -
we mourn for ourselves

To avoid misunderstandings I should explain that I am not questioning social norms, church laws or divine instructions to give anarchy its head. But it can well happen that in specific situations, people can only find their way to their inner selves and therefore to their inner equilibrium by daring to apply Jesus's words to themselves, according to which the sabbath was made for man and not man for the sabbath (Mk 2,27). And that means that they dare to be different from others.

The Point of the Story

From the point of view of depth psychology Luke's story about the healing of ten lepers is also about resisting the compulsion towards a perfection whose criteria are the work of men. According to the laws drawn up by men, they are entitled to judge others and condemn them. This interpretation which is quite legitimate, does not pose an alternative to a *theological* interpretation; it rather helps us to find our way towards it, and that implies smoothing the way towards the point the evangelist wishes to make. Once more let us listen to Jesus's command to "show yourselves to the priests!" As I have mentioned, lepers who were healed had to go to the priests who would then attest to their state through ritual cleansing. But the lepers that Jesus sends to the priests are not yet healed! Jesus tests their faith and so their trust in his word by commanding them to go to the priests and have their cleansing affirmed. It is only then, on their way, that they are freed from leprosy. Obviously all of them pass this test of faith and trust, as they are all healed.

The evangelist does not tell us whether the Samaritan fulfills his task, or whether he goes back to Jesus as soon as he is healed. Something else is important: the man who thanks God in a loud voice and falls on the ground before Jesus is a foreigner, above all a Samaritan.

Rabbi Eliezer who taught in 90 A.D. stated that: "He who eats the bread of Samaritans is like one who eats pork" (unclean). (Schebith VIII, 10).[9]

The Talmud is full of rabbinical discussions about how far a Jew may go in his dealings with Samaritans. The general tenor of the answers is, better have nothing to do with them. Jews and Samaritans were traditional enemies. This had historical reasons. In 721 B.C. Samaria, which lay between Galilee and Judea, was occupied by Assyria (2 Kings 17,5). The mixed race of the Samaritans sprang from the Israelites who remained in the country after the conquest, and the colonists who later settled there. When the Jews returned after the Babylonian captivity, they refused to help the Samaritans build a temple (Ezra 4,2). The Samaritans therefore erected their own temple in 5 B.C. on Mount Garizim (it was destroyed in 129 B.C.) This resulted in an independent Samaritan cult and religious practice. The breach was final. In contrast to the Jews, the Samaritans considered only the five books of Moses as holy scripture. Their hope for a Messiah rested on a prophet at the end of time, from whom they expected proclamation of the true teaching (Dtn 18,15-18; Jn 4,25).

The author of the book of Sirach (c.190 B.C.) had only contempt for the Samaritans: "with two nations my soul is vexed, and the third is no nation; those who live on Mount Seir and the Philistines, and the foolish people that dwell in Sechem" (Sir 50,25-26).

There are numerous references to this mutual hostility between Jews and Samaritans in ancient Jewish manuscripts, and also at Jesus's time. The Samaritans harried the Jews who had to cross through their territory if they wanted to make a pilgrimage to Jerusalem.[10]

After the Samaritans strewed bones of the dead in the Temple during the Passover feast, thus deliberately defiling the holy place, the hatred between the two peoples became irreconcilable. It is therefore clear that the story of the ten lepers makes a double theological statement.

Firstly we are dealing with the universality of the salvation that Jesus announces. Just as Naaman, who was not an Israelite but a Syrian, went back to thank Elisha, man of God, the Samaritan, not a believing Jew but a heretic, also goes back to Jesus to throw himself at his feet. The salvation that God dispenses is not limited to his chosen people - from the New Testament angle not limited to his Church - but is for all who seek him with honest hearts. *Besides,* Luke makes it clear that God himself turns towards mankind in Jesus's words and actions; it is expressly said that when the Samaritan is healed he praises "God with a loud voice" and gives Jesus thanks. Reginald Fuller has remarked that this is the whole point of the story; that it is not, as is often assumed, an exhortation to gratitude as such, but to the knowledge that one cannot honor God in any better way than by turning back to Jesus and thanking him.[11]

In its turn theological knowledge can be integrated into the depth psychological interpretation of the story. It is not the judges appointed by the institution (in Luke's language, the priests) or the conventions and regulations stipulated by them that have the last word about whether a man acts correctly or wrongly (biblically expressed, cleanly or uncleanly). The only relevant question is whether a man can answer for his actions to himself and to God because God is the only judge, and is above all human judges. Such belief can have a therapeutic function (religiously expressed, can bring about salvation). The consciousness that only God's judgement is decisive may be able—let us hope—to contribute to a person's gradually regaining self-confidence in a society or church that all too gladly play the part of the judge, and, according to their iron laws, are always tempted to slot people into the categories of evil and good, lepers and the healed, unclean and clean.

Perhaps this makes it clear to whom the question "Where are the nine?" is directed. The narrator puts this question into Jesus's mouth, thus turning to all who labor and are burdened. They must be encouraged to take the healed Samaritan as an example, for he alone gives honor to God and therefore does not have to worry about the judgement of others who cling to their human laws which have brought about so much injustice through their merciless use.

10
The Third Miracle

The Healing of Blind Bartimaeus (Mk 10,46-52)

What does a person do, who cannot go on anymore, who feels helpless, without strength, without power? Someone who cannot defend himself and does not know how to help himself? He screams out in fury, in hopelessness, out of total despair. And then last of all, perhaps, he screams out for help. That is, if he still has the strength.

Bertolt Brecht illustrates this in one of his "Stories of Mr Keuner" which is called "The Helpless Boy".

Mr K. talked about the bad habit of swallowing injustice silently, and told the following story. A man walking along asked a boy who was weeping to himself why he was so unhappy. I had two coins for the cinema said the boy, then another boy came along and snatched one of them out of my hand, and he pointed to a boy who could still be seen in the distance. Didn't you call out for help? asked the man. Yes, said the boy and sobbed a little louder. Didn't anyone hear you? asked the man again, stroking him gently. No, sobbed the boy. Can't you call out louder? asked the man. No, said the boy and looked at him with new hope. For the man was smiling. Then give me that, said he, and he took the last coin out of the boy's hand and went on quite unconcerned.

What is the moral behind this story? The action is quite

212

simple and correspondingly transparent. In any case we are justified in expecting the man to help the weeping boy because he smiles and strokes him lovingly. But then we learn that these are just his tactics. As soon as he finds out that he has nothing to fear because the boy cannot shout any louder, he robs him of the second coin and goes on his way, quite unconcerned.[1]

The two coins are a little fortune for the boy, for the man they are worth nothing. So why does he rob the boy instead of helping him? Or is he actually trying to help him on a long term basis in a cryptic but lasting way? Is he acting as a kind of teacher? If so, his seemingly unscrupulous behavior and his unconcerned departure could be a painful but necessary lesson for life, so to say: my dear boy, what you need is a special kind of voice training; as long as you are not capable of shouting out loudly you will always be a victim...

If we interpret the story in this way it goes against the grain. The man is not a pedagogue but a rascal, a cut-throat and an exploiter. He only robs the boy of his last coin after he is certain that he is helpless and weak.

However Brecht's narrator Mr Keuner (in fact Brecht himself) is of a pedagogical opinion. His message is: that's what it's like in life, it really is so brutal. If you don't know how to defend yourself, people will tear the coat off your back. If you behave like a moral coward you belong among the losers right from the beginning; if you show your weaknesses, you will go under.

The first sentence of the quotation tells us that this is Brecht's doctrine, and at the same time it is the key to understanding the whole story: "Mr K spoke about the bad habit of swallowing injustice", and the episode that follows really only tells us where this bad habit can lead. If you swallow everything you will remain a poor devil for ever. This is undoubtedly the moral of the story: you must never accept

213

the injustice that you suffer. Little acts of rebelliousness and half-hearted protests do nothing to improve the situation. It is much more important to shout out your fury and wrath for long enough to get help.

The Inability to come to Terms

Noisy, complaining people are burdensome. That is why we try to shut them up - either by giving way to them or stopping their mouths.
There is a healing miracle in Mark's gospel where both these alternatives are vividly described.

And (Jesus and his companions) came to Jericho; and as he was leaving Jericho with his disciples and a great multitude, Bartimaeus, a blind beggar, the son of Timaeus, was sitting by the roadside. And when he heard that it was Jesus of Nazareth, he began to cry out and say, "Jesus, Son of David, have mercy on me!" And many rebuked him, telling him to be silent; but he cried out all the more, "Son of David! Have mercy on me!" And Jesus stopped and said, "Call him." And they called the blind man, saying "Take heart; rise, he is calling you." And throwing off his mantle he sprang up and came to Jesus. And Jesus said to him "What do you want me to do for you?" And the blind man said to him "Master, let me receive my sight." And Jesus said to him "Go your way, your faith has made you well." And immediately he received his sight and followed him on the way (Mk 10,46-52).

The first readers of the story would have known at once what the evangelist wanted to say. He was concerned to announce Jesus as the Messiah. When Bartimaeus cries out to Jesus "Son of David, have mercy on me!" he is not only appearing as someone in need of help, but at the same time as witness and proclaimer of the belief that Jesus of Nazareth is indeed the promised Messiah. "Son of David" is a Jewish title for the Messiah that goes back to Nathan's prophesies (2 Sam 7,12-16) when the prophet proclaims to David in Yahweh's name "And your house and your kingdom shall be made sure for ever before me; your throne shall be established for ever" (7,16).

But at the same time Mark tells us in this episode that belief in Jesus as the Messiah will only reach fulfillment when it shows results, or to be more precise, when it leads to *successors or followers* of Jesus. In order to support this argument we must dig a little deeper.

According to the evangelist, on his way which led from Galilee towards the south through Judea to Jerusalem and from there to Golgotha, Jesus and his disciples go to the oasis town of Jericho. We know nothing more about their stay there except that in the end numerous inhabitants of the town go with Jesus and his disciples to Jerusalem. At the edge of the town they come upon a blind beggar, and in contrast to many others who are healed by Jesus, the evangelist introduces him by name: Bar Timaeus (son of Timaeus).

This blind man has always wanted to have his sight back, but naturally he knows that this is wishful thinking. That is why he has learned to fit into his role. For years he has like other beggars whined and complained, because it is expected of him. He has to take what he is given, if indeed he gets anything. He has to be happy about anything he gets, and he is probably very happy about each little bit. For he is actually looked after. He just has to come to terms with his lot and what he gets. The donations are the payments with which his fellow citizens buy a good conscience. As a beggar however Bartimaeus has no right to any financial aid and none at all to human care. That is why his whining has to be kept within clearly defined limits. Somehow all this is understood. If his

215

conduct is too obstreperous, he has to reckon with people letting him know about it. This alone is enough to prevent him from shouting out loudly and clearly what he has felt for years: I'm a human being too! Presumably people would put him in his place again, alms would be sparse, and anyway, Bartimaeus already takes into account that he is not a human being but a *beggar*, completely helpless and dependent upon others for the smallest of morsels. What is the point of resisting? Why not just go on fitting in?

In this kind of circumstance every protest seems useless. And this quite apart from the fact that he would need help from outside. How can one overcome that sense of shame that society, one's own relations included, have inflicted upon one without obtaining aid from elsewhere?

It is often much harder to let oneself be helped than to help. A person who does not know how to help himself anymore feels humiliated and degraded. He is dependent upon others and completely and utterly at their mercy. They can tread on him or grind him into the ground. That is why he does not trust himself to admit publicly to his acute need. At most he sends out a signal or two, but these are mostly not noticed.

One has to accept one's lot - that had been Bartimaeus's experience over the years. He knows that his existence is no life, and what he is given only just makes it possible for him to survive. When he hears about Jesus and his works he becomes conscious that things could be different. And now he hears that this Jesus is passing by, and the miracle happens. The beggar begins to shout with all his might. And immediately those who find this impertinent start resisting him. For these people have also come to terms with the situation. Their contributions support Bartimaeus and therefore they have the right to be left in peace. And because things have their order, and (this above all!) disturbances are not to be tolerated under any circumstances, they shout at the beggar and order him to be quiet. But Bartimaeus shouts even louder, so loud that Bertolt Brecht would have been absolutely delighted.

Indirectly this shouting aims at the freedom that Bartimaeus has secretly always longed for and yet feared. If Jesus heals him, from one moment to the next he will have to do without the care of his fellow countrymen, and will be left entirely to his own resources. The new chances in life that he had hoped for also have their threatening side.

However he shouts at Jesus, who opens his eyes, and the blind man sees again, but quite differently and seeing different things from what he had expected. This is because he deliberately ignores Jesus's command "Go your way" and does not go back into the town but follows Jesus on his way.

And this is what the story amounts to! For Bartimaeus has never for a moment thought of this possibility. He had simply - and firmly - reckoned that Jesus could heal him from his infirmity. And it follows from Jesus's last remark: "Your faith has made you well."

Following the Cross

In understanding this story it is important to mention that it does not end with Jesus's words, but with a remark from the evangelist: And Bartimaeus "followed him on the way." This means the way of Jesus, which after Jerusalem leads him to the place of his suffering; from now on Bartimaeus is one of Jesus's disciples.

And now the evangelist conceives of the *whole way* of Jesus from Galilee into the city as a "way of the cross" which will only be completed at Golgotha. According to Mark following Jesus is also always following the cross. And *this* is implied when it is said of Bartimaeus (it has already been said of the apostles; Mk 1,17-20; 2,14) that he follows Jesus on his way. It is not by chance that Mark puts the following words into Jesus's mouth exactly two chapters before the Bartimaeus story: "If any man would come after me, let him deny himself and take up his cross and follow me" (Mk 8,34).

In their present form these words obviously originated after Easter; they are not a historical but a theological statement. They presuppose Jesus's death on the cross without which they would be completely incomprehensible. They express the fact that every true following of Jesus includes the readiness to suffer *in the sense that Jesus did.*

But these words about following the cross have often been interpreted in the Christian tradition in a way that misses the point of Jesus's suffering, in the sense that it is sometimes held that the Christian is bound to *seek* suffering, which practically equals denial for the sake of denial. This kind of mystical suffering has nothing to do with following Jesus; it can be fitted more easily into the area of psychopathology.

The only criterion for following the cross (and, linked to it, the readiness to suffer) is signified in the example of Jesus. Jesus did not seek suffering, but fought against all pain. It was not his wish to die on the cross. He begged God in tears to save him from this terrible fate (Mk 14,36). All his life he fought against the pain he encountered by forgiving sinners, by taking sides with the weak, and by eating meals with people that others thought of as rejected by God.

Jesus remained true to his mission although, at least at the end of his public life, he knew that he was risking his life in doing so. *This* pain that comes from commitment to the disadvantaged and the weak was what he expected from his disciples. Whenever they remained true to his example they were of necessity placed into conflict with those who always have their own advantages at heart and never the well-being of their fellow men.

Following the cross means: do not ignore suffering but work through it. What is meant here are those quite personal experiences that are a heavy burden: a terrible past, oppressive guilt, failure that cannot be made good. One is so often tempted in such situations to escape into forgetfulness or repression.

Here is what following the cross means: work at whatever is oppressive or difficult, confront it in thoughts, in talks with friends, in the face of God. That is an extremely stressful process, or put in Christian terms, a cross that is laid upon one. But a person comes out of such suffering liberated, enlightened and mature.

Finally, following the cross can also imply carrying pain. I mean that pain which is stronger and greater than all one's possibilities - for example, incurable disease, an inescapable situation, the death of a beloved person. Followers of Jesus try to accept such pain in that they pray like Jesus and with him, "Abba, Father—yet not what I will, but what thou wilt" (Mk 14,36).

Understood in this way, following Jesus and the cross can be best described by the concept "Martyrium". This Greek expression *martys, (martyros), martyria (martyrion) martyrein* means witness, evidence and to testify. The first person to seal his evidence of Jesus with his blood was Stephen the Deacon (Acts 22,20; 6,7-8, 60). *This* martyrdom as acceptance of Jesus's death and thereby as an extreme act of love (Jn 15,13) forms the case where the real thing happens and the borderline case in every following of Jesus. The real thing happens in so far as the conditionless following of Jesus involves readiness to testify to Jesus to the bitter end, even at the price of one's own life. And the borderline case covers most disciples of Jesus who are not subjected to this test by blood.

But there is certainly no authentic following of Jesus

without the readiness to accept martyrdom. As a rule this dedication of one's life to Jesus and his works happens in actively following him which, according to Paul's experience, signifies a life-long process of dying: "I have been crucified with Christ; it is no longer I who live, but Christ who lives in me" (Gal 2,19; Rom 6,3-11).

It would be a crude misunderstanding to confuse this following as *imitation*. Following happens in real situations, which have to be understood and overcome constantly in faith. Expressed differently, it is about trying to re-form the respective individual and social realities of life to correspond to Jesus's instruction and example.

The first miracle that the story of Bartimaeus tells us is that the blind man finds the courage to shout against the superior strength of those who think differently, and to get himself a hearing. The second miracle happens when he *lets* his eyes be opened, and goes the unusual way that stretches out quite astonishingly before him. Finally, the third miracle happens every and each time a person takes this story to his heart and decides to follow.

FOOTNOTES

PART ONE
RECORDS OF MIRACLES IN RELIGIONS

1
THE BLIND SEE, THE LAME WALK
AND THE DEAD RISE

1. Bruce Marshall. Father Malachy's Miracle.

2. R. Herzog, Die Wunderheilungen von Epidauros; ein Beitrag zur Geschichte der Medizin und der Religion. Quoted by A. Weiser, die Apostelgeschichte (Okumenischer Taschenbuch Kommentar zum Neuen Testament, vol. 5/1) Gütersloh und Würzburg, 1981, 141.

3. G. Theißen, Urchristliche Wundergeschichten, (Studien zum Neuen Testament, vol. 8) Gütersloh (1974, 98). Theißen's typology of miracles is now widely accepted.

4. This story is handed down by Philostratus, Vita Apollinii, iv, 45; quoted by A. Weiser, Was die Bibel Wunder nennt, Stuttgart, 1975, 127; more on this in ch. 4 of this book.

5. The Book of Tobit is not counted among the canonical manuscripts in Judaism (see Hebrew Bible in Special Terms at the end of this book).

6. H. Gressmann (ed.) Altorientalische Texte zum Alten Testament, Berlin, Leipzig, 1926, 78f.

7. Josephus Flavius, Jewish Antiquities, VIII, 2, 5, quoted by A. Weiser, Was die Bibel Wunder nennt, Stuttgart, 1975, 83 f.

8. Herzog, quoted by Weiser, Apostelgeschichte, 142.

9. Further examples of punitive miracles from Judaism and the Greek-Hellenistic environment in Weiser, Apostelgeschichte, 139-142.

10. Porphyry, Life of Pythagoras, 25; quoted by Theißen.

11. Babylonian Talmud, tract Baba Mezia, 59b; quoted from "Der Talmud," selected, translated, and explained by R. Mayer, (Goldmann Klassiker, vol. 7571) Munich, 1986, 313.

12. For more detail, see J. Imbach, The Three Faces of Jesus: How Jews, Christians and Muslims See Him. Templegate Publishers, 1992.

13. The Babylonian Talmud, Traktat Berakhot; quoted from "Der Talmud," ausgewählt, intersetzt und erklärt by R. Meyer (Goldmann Klassiker, vol. 7571) Munich, 1986, 433.

14. The Jerusalem Talmud, Traktat Berakhot ix, 1. Quoted from Weiser, Wunder, 109. There are numerous references to miracles of rescue from shipwreck in the Hellenistic world in R. Pesch, Das Markusevangelium. Pt I (Herder Theological Commentary on the New Testament, vol. 2.) Freiburg, Basle, Vienna, 1976, 274.

15. Quoted from Weiser, Wunder, 176.

16. After Weiser, 105-119.

2
MIRACLES ACCEPTED YESTERDAY

1. R. Bultmann, Neues Testament und Mythologie, in: H.W. Bartsch (ed.) Kerygma und Mythos, vol. 1. Hamburg-Bergstedt, 1960, 16.
2. H. Denzinger, Kompendium der Glaubensbekenntnisse und kirchlichen Lehrentscheidungen. Verbessert, erweitert, ins Deutsche übertragen und unter Mitarbeit von Helmut Hoping; herausgegeben von Peter Hünermann, Freiburg, Basle, Rome, Vienna, 1991 (Latin/German) 822 f (no. 3034) Future references abbreviated to DH with document number.
3. DH 3009.
4. dtv Lexikon, vol. 20. Munich, 1973, 119.
5. Berthold Brecht, The Mother, from Works, vol. 5. tr. from the German by Jane Wilde.
6. B. Weissmahr, Natürliche Phänomene und Wunder in; F. Böckle (ed.) Christlicher Glaube in moderner Gesellschaft, vol. 4. Freiburg, Basle, Vienna 1982. For following also compare 121-148.
7. Augustine, Contra Faustum, 29, 4; in PL 42, 207-518; here 490: "contra natura cursum notissimum"; compare 26, 3, ebd. 480 f.
8. In 1713 Pope Clement XI condemned a number of errors made by the French theologian Pasquier Quesnel (1643-1719), including the sentence that "no grace can be granted outside the church." See also DH 2419.
9. Vatican II. Account of the relationship of the Church to non-Christian religions, Nostra aetate, no. 2.

3
FAITH'S DEAREST CHILD

1. The example from Epidaurus is quoted by A. Weiser in Was die Bibel Wunder nennt, Stuttgart, 1975, 41.
2. For more on this see J. Imbach, Die Bibel lesen und verstehen, Munich 1986; W. Kasper, Jesus der Christus, Mainz 1992, esp. 75-188; Geschichte und Geschick Jesu Christi. Zur historischen Frage nach den Wundern.
3. B. Wenisch, Geschichten oder Geschichte? Theologie des Wunders, Salzburg 1981, 5.
4. R. Pesch Jesu ureigene Taten? (Questiones disputatae, vol. 52.) Freiburg, Basle, Vienna, 1970, 143. Italics are mine.
5. Augustine, Tractus in Joannis Evangelium, 24, 1, in PL 35, 1379-1975; here 1593.
6. Vatican II. Dogmatic Constitution on Divine Revelation, Dei Verbum, no. 3.
7. J.W. von Goethe, Faust I, v. 766

Part Two
MIRACLES FROM THE NEW TESTAMENT

1
SINKING IN THE VOID

1. Jean Paul, "Siebenkäs" in Works, vol 1. Berlin, Darmstadt, Vienna 1962 609-1158, the "Speech of the Dead Christ" 890-894. tr. Jane Wilde.

2. Ebd, 894, & the following quotation 890.

3. Thérèse of Lisieux, Autobiography, Einsiedeln, 1991, 14; 3; 7. This autobiography is composed of three different parts: 1) Memories of childhood 2) a personal letter to Sister Marie du Sacre-Coeur, her eldest sister and godmother, also a Carmelite nun in Lisieux 3) a continuation of childhood memories and reflections on life in the convent. Previously these notebooks were published under the title "The Story of a Soul."

4. After Thérèse's canonization the following statement by one of the sisters was released: "These doubts were above all concerned with the existence of heaven. She did not talk to anyone about them, as she did not want to pass on her unspeakable torment. She would have gladly trusted in a father confessor, but our chaplain was near to confusing her, in that he told her her state of mind was very dangerous."

5. H.V. von Balthasar, Preface to "Thérèse von Lisieux, Autobiographie."

6. See V. Luz, Das Evangelium nach Matthäus, 2. Teilband, Mt. 8-17. (Evangelisch-Katholischer Kommentar zum Neuen Testament, vol. 1/2) Zürich, Braunschweig, Neukirchen-Vluyn 1990, 407.

7. Jatakas are stories from Buddha's early life. The collection dating from the fifth century is based on essentially older (partly pre-Christian) traditions. The following quotation (Jataka 190) in J.B. Aufhauser, Buddha und Jesus. Bonn, 1926, 12. Other examples of walking on the water are also found here.

8. A. Andersch, Sansibar oder der letzte grund. (Fischer Bücherei, vol. 354)

9. Vatican II. Dogmatic Constitution on the Church. Lumen Gentium. no. 9.

10. Vatican II. Ecumenical Decree Unitatis redintegratio, no. 3.

2
LAW OR JUSTICE

1. Friedrich Dürrenmatt, Monstervortrag über Gerechtigkeit und Recht, Zürich 1969, 115-119. Tr: Jane Wilde.

2. Compare H.L. Strack/P. Billerbeck, Kommentar zum Neuen Testament aus Talmud und Midrasch, vol. I: Das Evangelium nach Matthäus, Munich, 1965, 615-631.

3. General Synod of Bishops in the Federal Republic of Germany; Marriage and the Family in official edition, vol I Freiburg, Basle, Vienna, 1976, 452.

4. Synod 72 of the Diocese of Basle. Marriage and Family in Our Changing Society (nos. 7,8) Solothurn, 1974 31-33. The following quotation also comes from this.

3
"YOU GIVE THEM SOMETHING TO EAT!"

1. Compare H.L. Strack/P. Billerbeck, Kommentar zum Neuen Testament aus Talmud und Midrasch, vol 2: Das Evangelium nach Markus, Lukas und Johannes und die Apostelgeschichte, Munich 1961, 483 f.

2. Georges Bernanos. The Diary of a Country Priest. Macmillan, 1937. tr: Pamela Morris.

3. A. Schilling, Was die Kirche krank macht. Regensburg, 1992, 25.

4. P. Manns (ed.) Die Heiligen, Mainz, 1975, 555.

5. L. Zenetti, Sieben Farben hat das Licht. Munich, 1981, 116.

223

4
OF DEVILS, DEMONS AND EVIL SPIRITS

1. D.F. Strauß, Das Leben Jesu für das deutsche Volk bearbeitet, vol. 2. Bonn, 1891, 183; H. Gunkel, Das Märchen im Alten Testament, Tübingen, 1926, 87; R. Bultmann, Die Geschichte der synoptischen Tradition (1921) Göttingen 1967, 225; B. Russell "Why I am not a Christian."
2. Compare R. Pesch, Der Besessene von Gerasa. Entstehung und Überlieferung einer Wundergeschichte (Stuttgarter Bibelstudien, vol. 56) Stuttgart 1972, 18.
3. J. Gnilka, Das Evangelium nach Markus (Evangelisch-Katholischer Kommentar zum Neuen Testament, vol. II/1) Zürich, Einsiedeln, Cologne und Neukirchen-Vluyn, 1978, 207.
4. W. Schmithals, Das Evangelium nach Markus (Ökumenischer Taschenbuch Kommentar zum Neuen Testament, vol. II/1, Gütersloh 1979, 266. The following interpretation is partly based on this commentary.
5. See H. Haag et al. Teufelsglaube, Tübingen 1974, 141-217.
6. M. Limbeck, Satan und das Böse im Neuen Testament, in: Haag, 317.
7. More about this in R. Kieckhefer, Magic im Mittelalter, Munich 1992, 19; 84-91. In the Middle Ages, bodily afflictions were also blamed on evil gnomes and elves, as well as on demons.
8. F.M. Dostoevsky "The Possessed", Heinemann, 1946. Excerpts to follow translated from the German by Jane Wilde.
9. Schmithals, 268.
10. The plea for some concession in accounts of banishing demons is almost as frequent as the "Amen" in the church, see Pesch, 34: "As an element of exorcism it comes from the Egyptian tradition, and is then taken over in Jewish and Hellenistic miracle stories"
11. See Pesch, 37f: "Worm your way into the head of the bull, there eat his flesh, drink his blood, destroy his eyes, fill his head with darkness....Give the pig instead of him, give him its flesh as his flesh, its blood as his blood, let him take this. Give him its heart as his heart, and let him take it."
12. Schmithals, 280.

5
"IT IS NOT I WHO ACT"

1. F. Mauriac, "A Woman of the Pharisees." London Eyre and Spottiswoode, 1949. tr. Gerard Hopkins.
2. "Das Neue Testament" Übersetzt von F. Stier, Munich und Düsseldorf, 1989.
3. See K.P. Fischer/H. Schiedermair, Die Sache mit dem Teufel, Frankfurt a.M. 1980, 173 f.
4. ibid. 174 f.
5. Origen, Comment. in Matthaeum, Tomus XIII in: P.G. 13, 1106f; quoted by R. Pesch, das Markus-evangelium, pt. II (Herders theologischer Kommentar zum Neuen Testament) Frieburg, Basle, Vienna, 1977, 89. (Pesch does not give the correct source; commentary to Mt. 13, 6 instead of 17,15).
6. see Pesch, 95.
7. E. Vittorini, "Men and Not Men," translated by Sarah Henry, Marlboro Press, Marlboro VT, 1985.

8. L. Tolstoy, "Resurrection," tr. from the German by J.W.
9. B. Pascal, "Thoughts," fragment 140. tr. from the German by J.W.
10. J.W. von Goethe, Faust, Pt I. v. 112

6
POUR OUT GOOD WINE

1. The healing of the son of an official (Jn 4, 46-54); The healing of the sick man at the pool of Bethesda (Jn 5, 1-9); The feeding of the five thousand (6, 1-13); Jesus walks on the Sea of Galilee (6, 16-21); Healing of the Blind Man (9, 1-34); The raising of Lazarus (11, 1-44).
2. Compare H.L. Strack/P. Billerbeck, Kommentar zum Neuen Testament aus Talmud und Midrasch, vol. I: Das Evangelium nach Matthias, Munich 1965, 517; and to the following 616, f.
3. See R. Schnackenburg, Das Johannes Evangelium, pt I (Herders theologischer Kommentar zum Neuen Testament) Freiburg, Basle, Vienna, 1967, 343.
4. Compare the Feeding of the Five Thousand (Mk 6, 32-44); the Feeding of the Four Thousand (Mk 8, 1-10); Peter's miraculous catch of Fish (Lk 5, 1-11).
5. For what follows see R.H. Fuller, Die Wunder Jesu in Exegese und Verkündigung, Düsseldorf 1967, 107.
6. Quoted by A. Steiner/A. Weymann, Wunder Jesu. Bibelarbeit in der Gemeinde, Basle, Zürich, Cologne, 1978.
7. Catechismus ex decreto Concilii Tridentini ad parochos, Rome 1858 (1566). The first Catholic catechism (from the Council of Trent) was the Roman reply to Luther's "Großem Katechismus" (1530). It was written in Latin, and designed to serve the clergy as a basic handbook for proclaiming the faith.
8. F. Nietzsche "Also sprach Zarathustra" pt 2. "Von großen Ereignissen."
9. A. Exeler, Gott, der uns entgegenkommt. Freiburg i. Br. 1980, 46.
10. Vatican II, Dogmatic Constitution of the Church, Lumen gentium, no 9. Italics are mine.
11. Vatican II. Decree on Ecumenism, Unitatis redintegratio, no. 3.
12. Vatican II. Pastoral Constitution on the Church in the world of today, Gaudium et spes, no. 1.

7
SAY YES TO YOURSELF

1. See page 39 of this book.
2. See J. Gnilka, das Evangelium nach Markus (Evangelisch-Katholischer Kommentar zum Neuen Testament, vol. II/1/ Zürich, Einsiedeln, Cologne und Neukirchen-Vluyn, 1978, 97f.
3. Thomas Mann, Letters 1889-1936. Frankfurt a. Main. 1961, 125.
4. Compare W. Schmithals, Das Evangelium nach Markus, (Ökumenischer Taschenbuch Kommentar zum Neuen Testament 2/1) Gütersloh und Würzburg, 1979, 158.
5. Leo Tolstoy, "Resurrection" tr. from the German by J.W.
6. C. Vogel, Il peccatore e la penitenza nel Medioevo, Turin, 1970, 62 & 66.

8
STANDING ON YOUR OWN FEET

1. B. Pascal, Pensées. Fragment 425. tr. from German by J.W.
2. Philostratos, Vita Apollinii IV, 45, quoted by A. Weiser, Was die Bibel Wunder nennt. Stuttgart, 1975, 127.
3. Passages in bold in both stories are mine.
4. Compare H.L. Strack/P. Billerbeck, Kommentar zum Neuen Testament aus Talmud und Midrasch. vol I: Das Evangelium nach Matthäus, Munich 1965, 560.
5. The following considerations were inspired by E. Drewermann, Und legte ihnen die Hände auf. Predigten über die Wunder Jesu. ed. B. Marz, Düsseldorf 1993, 146-151.
6. M. Frisch, Stiller, tr. from the German by J.W.

9
REJECTED, EXCLUDED, BANISHED

1. For the following, R. Pesch, Jesu ureigene Taten? Ein Beitrag zur Wunderfrage. (Quaestiones Disputatae, vol. 52) Freiburg, Basle, Vienna, 1970, 114-134.
2. For further examples of adding numbers, page 44 in this book under heading "From the History of Jesus to History with Jesus"
3. See Pesch, 127.
4. H. L. Strack/P. Billerbeck. Kommentar zum Neuen Testament aus Talmud und Midrasch, vol IV/2. Exkurse zu einzelnen Stellen des Neuen Testaments, Munich 1961, 723-45. ("Aussatz und Aussätzige;" dort auch die weiteren Hinweise); the quotation, 753.
5. ebd. 753
6. E. Drewermann, Zwischen Staub und Sternen, Predigten im Jahreskreis, Düsseldorf, 1991, 205.
7. ebd. 206
8. K. Marti, Leichenreden (Lizenzauzgabe ex libris), Zurich o.J., 121.
9. See Strack/Billerbeck, Kommentar (compare Anm. 4), vol. I: Das Evangelium nach Markus, Munich 1965, 542.
10. See, apart from Luke, Josephus Flavius, Jüdische Altertümer, 20, 6; the following episode ebd. 18, 3. For uncleanliness through dead bodies, see Num. 19, 11-16.
11. R. H. Fuller. The Miracles of Jesus in Exegesis and Proclamation.

10
THE THIRD MIRACLE

1. B. Brecht, Geschichten vom Herrn Keuner, in: Gesammelte Werke, vol. 12, Frankfurt a.M. 1967, 381. tr. from the German by J.W.

SPECIAL TERMS

ANATHEMA: see Excommunication.

APOTHEGM: a word from the Greek meaning pithy saying or maxim. Bible interpreters applied it to a New Testament story which was structured round one of Jesus's important and weighty statements (Mk 3,1-6).

CALIPH: Title of the successors to Muhammad who ruled over the entire Islamic community. In 1517 the Caliphate changed into the Sultanate (rule) of Constantinople. As a result of the national revival in Turkey after the First World War both the Sultanate (1922) and the Caliphate (1924) were abolished.

CANON, CANONICAL: all the writings in the Bible form the *Canon* (the Holy Scriptures). This is why we also speak of the *canonical scriptures*. By the word canon in Roman Catholic Church law (the codex of canonical law) we understand legal regulations systematically divided into paragraphs.

CHORAL ENDING OR CADENCE: this term, taken from music, especially referring to the final choruses in J.S. Bach's works, can often be applied to the miracle stories of the first three evangelists. It is the astonished words of praise for Jesus's miracles, voiced by those present. The account of the healing of the paralytic, for example, finishes with the sentence: "...they were all amazed and glorified God, saying, 'We never saw anything like this!'" (Mk 2,12).

CHRISTOLOGY: teaching of the person of Christ which was conceptually developed during the course of the dogmatic debates of early Christianity.

COUNCIL DOCUMENTS OF VATICAN II: Vatican II has 16 documents which are described by their titles (i.e. Lumen gentium).
We distinguish between three categories of text:
4 Constitutions: basic statements enlarging the teaching and practice of faith;
9 Decrees: resolutions and instructions for practical questions (for example, the position of the laity or the church's missionary activities);
3 Explanations: these also refer to specific questions (for example, the significance of non-christian religions). However, they sketch out the problems rather than suggest a definite solution.

EXCOMMUNICATION: the expulsion from the Church community of a baptized Christian for wrongful behavior or false teaching, thereby banning him or her from receiving the sacraments.

EXEGESIS: the exposition of scripture, upon which the meaning of statements and the sense of a text are based. It relies upon various methods: see the history of form, of editing and of tradition.

THE GRAND VIZIER: the prime minister in Islamic monarchies.

HEBREW BIBLE: this corresponds to the Old Testament scriptures recognized by the *Roman Catholic Church* as binding, with the exceptions of the Books of Judith, Tobit, the First and the Second Books of the Maccabees, Wisdom, Sirach and Baruch. Also the Hebrew Bible does not include the additions to the Book of Esther written in Greek, or the additions to the Book of Daniel. In contrast, *the Churches of the Reformation* hold to the first (Old) Testament of the Hebrew Bible.

HELLENISM: this describes the mixed culture of Oriental and Greek elements that arose after Alexander the Great (356-323 B.C.). It influenced life in the Greek colonies and the areas surrounding these. At the time of Jesus, Palestine had been under Hellenistic rule and the culture resulting from it for a good 360 years (see 2 Macc 4,13). It is therefore not surprising that Hellenism had a profound influence on Judaism and Christianity. Its epoch came to an end c. 200 A.D.

HISTORY OF EDITING: this attempts to establish at what point of history the biblical authors selected oral and written traditions, put them together and worked them into their writings.

HISTORY OF FORM: this describes the various literary forms (e.g. simile, parable, miracle story) and genres (letter, chronicle, gospel) which were used by the authors of the Holy Scriptures.

HISTORY OF TRADITION: this is the study of the historical transmission of original texts and narratives. It researches the various phases of the oral and written handing down of a text (e.g. of a parable) beginning with its origins to the final written account within a biblical book.

IMAM: Prayer leader in the mosque.

KORAN: The sacred text of the Muslims. It consists of 114 Suras (chapters) which, similar to the Bible, are divided into verses.

PAROUSIA: the second coming of Christ. The Hebrew Bible constantly speaks of *the Day of Yahweh or the Day of the Lord*. In using this concept the *prophets* thought mainly of God's future judgement of Israel, from which the people would emerge enlightened and revenged upon their enemies (Mal 3,2; Zech 12, 1-20). Later the *apocalyptic* concept of "The Day of the Lord" was in agreement with the prophetic vision in that the change for the better would take place in *this* world. All injustice would be overcome, so that peace and justice could reign over mankind ever after. It was later that the "Day of Yahweh's Judgement" became linked to the coming *End of the World* (Dan 9,26; 12,13), when one would appear "as the Son of Man" (Dan 7,13f). Jesus had this concept, and it was taken over by the early Christian Church and modified at the same time. The expected Son of Man was then identified with Christ, whose *parousia* (second coming) was originally expected immediately.

PERICOPE: a paragraph of a biblical text which is read aloud or used as a theme for preaching during divine service. It is liturgically determined.

RABBI: in the Talmud and the New Testament the word means "master" or "teacher". The form of address *rabbi* developed into an honorary title, which was given to the Palestinian teachers of the law after the first century A.D.

The great Jewish teachers of the past were all called rabbi, while the Jewish representatives of the community were called rabbins. Their position can be compared to that of a parson or preacher in the Protestant Free Church.

SURA: see Koran.

SYNOPTICS: description of the evangelists Matthew, Mark and Luke, whose gospels complement each other to a large extent, thus forming a synopsis (a common view).

TALMUD: The Talmud (literally, the Study) is a collection of laws and religious records of post-biblical Judaism, which developed during the time c. 200 B.C. to roughly 500 A.D. In the outer form of the text one distinguishes between the *Mishnah* ("repetition," which is the teaching of the fathers, learnt by being repeated sentence by sentence), and the *Gemara* (completion of the teaching or commentaries by later teachers). The inner form of the Talmud, however, divides into the *Halacha* and the *Haggada*. The Halacha (way of life) contains the laws—guides, decisions of the masters, the passing on of traditional customs—and takes up about two-thirds of the book. The Haggada (narration) includes narrative collections, i.e. proverbs, parables, legends, anecdotes. The whole Talmud consists of six main portions or rules (agriculture, feast times, marriage law, civil and criminal law, holy objects, ritual cleansing instructions), which in their turn are divided into single tracts.

There are two versions of the Talmud named according to their place of origin: the Palestinian (Jerusalem) and the Babylonian Talmud—when speaking simply of the Talmud, the latter more comprehensive version is usually implied.

TORAH: Hebrew word for "instruction" or "law" (of

God): in a narrower sense in ancient Judaism it is comprised of the five books of Moses (Genesis, Exodus,Leviticus, Numbers, Deuteronomy); in a wider sense the whole of the Hebrew Testament, and frequently the whole of Jewish religious law.

TRANSCENDENT: that which surpasses the boundaries of human experience and imagination. Speaking of God's transcendence implies his "beyond the worldness" and his "difference from the world". God is simply greater than all that man can think or say of him.

YHWH: the most usual name for God in the Hebrew Bible. In this book (as in the German Ecumenical translation of the Holy Scriptures) vowels are added to the four consonants of the tetragram (Greek *tetra* = four, *gramma* = letter) YHWH. The Jews have such great reverence for the name YHWH that they do not speak it.

Index of Names

I have not included biblical names in this list because they are so frequently mentioned.